SECRETARY'S HANDBOOK

Vera and Christina Hughes

TEACH YOURSELF BOOKS

Hodder and Stoughton

First published 1988
Second impression 1989

British Library Cataloguing in Publication Data
Hughes, Vera
Secretary's handbook.—(Teach yourself
books).
1. Office practice
I. Title   II. Hughes, Christina
651   HF5547.5

ISBN 0 340 41763 3

Printed and bound in Great Britain
for Hodder and Stoughton Educational,
a division of Hodder and Stoughton Ltd,
Mill Road Dunton Green Sevenoaks, Kent,
by Richard Clay Ltd,
Bungay, Suffolk
Photoset by Rowland Phototypesetting Ltd,
Bury St Edmunds, Suffolk

This volume is available in the USA from
Random House, Inc.,
201 East 50th Street, M.D. 4–6, New York, N.Y. 10022

CONTENTS

PREFACE

This book is a reference book. It is intended to be used by anyone who works in an office, but especially by secretaries and aspiring secretaries.

Unit 1 deals with secretarial skills and procedures, and will be useful to people who have not previously taken on the tasks performed by a personal secretary. It assumes basic knowledge and skills, such as typewriting, word processing and audio, and how to use the telephone, and sets out the things you will need to think about if you are suddenly faced with making appointments, keeping a diary etc. It is for quick reference, and is not a substitute for sound training in these skills and procedures.

The rest of the book covers defined subject areas and sets out under each, as briefly as possible, the main points you may need to know, and where to go for further information. The authors have tried to put into the book all the things they have found people want to look up, but do not know where to start; not every detail on every subject is included, but the book should give some ideas and pointers about where to go next if the precise and detailed information is not there. This book does not presume to deal with all the subject matter covered in good secretarial and office practice books. It is, we say again, intended to be a *reference* book. The next section – 'How to use this book' – will help you use it as such.

The authors have made every effort to verify the information in this book which, at the time of publication, is correct as far as they are aware.

HOW TO USE THIS BOOK

As this is a reference book, it is designed to enable you to look things up quickly and easily.

How to find a topic quickly

The book is divided into 12 main *Units*, in alphabetical order except the first and the last.

1 Secretarial Skills and Procedures
2 Communication
3 The Electronic Office and Telecommunications
4 Health and Safety at Work
5 Legal Matters
6 Meetings and Conferences
7 Money, Banking and Finance
8 Organisation Structure
9 Stationery
10 Trading Documents and Procedures
11 Travel
12 General Information

Each Unit is divided into *sections* (and *sub-sections*), and the *Contents* pages give an outline of what each Unit contains. The sections within each Unit are in alphabetical order. So if you want to study, or look up, a certain topic (say, Credit cards), then look in the Contents pages under **7 Money, Banking and Finance** and you will find the section number for Credit cards. Then, to help you to locate the section you are looking for as quickly as possible, there is a box at the top right hand corner of each right-hand page, giving a brief listing of the sections on that page and the page opposite.

Use the Index

If you want specific *detail* about a topic, turn to the Index at the back of the book, and try to find a word which best describes the reference you want.

For example, if you wanted to know what insurance cover is given when you hire a car, you might think of looking under 'Car hire' or under 'Insurance'. If you look under 'Car hire' in the Index:

you; co-operation between manager and secretary is essential.

Check diaries first thing every morning, and several times during the day. Check diaries particularly:

- after meetings, when date of next meeting might have been agreed;
- after telephone calls;
- in conjunction with correspondence in and out of the office, including internal memos.

1.2.2   Relevant information

Agree with your manager the details which should be written in the diary for different types of appointment *(See 1.1)*.

Note *at least*:
- name of person/people to be seen
- time of appointment
- venue

Add, if required:
- subject of meeting
- relevant telephone numbers

1.2.3   One diary for two managers

Keep entries in columns which can be crossed for joint appointments

		Mr A	*Miss B*
TUESDAY			
10	1000	Management Committee Room 101	
	1030		Meeting with Press Conference Room A
	1100		
	1130	Briefing meeting for Sales Conference Conference Room B	

1.2.4   Personal entries

Some people like to keep personal entries in their office diaries, e.g. dentist, daughter's birthday, dinner and dance. It can be useful to write this type of entry in a different colour, or in pencil.

1.3   Filing

You will normally be following an established filing system; whether you are creating your own system or keeping up-to-date with one you have inherited, the ultimate test of any system is: 'Can I find it?', and even more crucial: 'Can *other people* find it?'

1.2 Diaries
1.3 Filing

1.3.1 Creating a system

If you have to create a filing system, consider the following:

Which classification?
- Alphabetical: by client, customer etc., in alphabetical order.
- Numerical: by client, customer etc. being allocated a file number each.
- Geographic: by region, area, town etc., and then alphabetically.
- Subject: by subject matter (e.g. sales, purchases, personnel, etc.), and then alphabetically.

Choose the classification most appropriate to your work.

Which storage equipment?
- Filing cabinets, cupboards, special circular containers, etc.
- Microfilm, microfiche readers and containers
- Card index containers

Which materials?
- Manilla folders, hanging files, box files, loose-leaf files etc.
- Index cards etc.
- Filing flags or tabs
- Microfilm or microfiche materials

Details of several possibilities are given in *Teach Yourself Secretarial Practice* and many other office practice books.

1.3.2 Where to put it

Mis-filing is the main cause of losing information. Some rules for awkward alphabetical filing are:

- If a reference contains *two or more names*, file under the first and cross-reference under the others if necessary, e.g. Latter & Small, file under 'Latter' and cross-reference under 'Small'.
- For *hyphenated double-barrelled names* file under the first name, e.g. Main-Brown: file under 'M'.

- For *double-barrelled names* which are *not hyphenated* file under the second name, e.g. Main Brown: file under 'B'.
- Ignore words such as 'The', 'a' and 'an' in English, and foreign company titles such as 'Société', 'Firma' etc., particularly if they precede the company name.
- *St or Saint*: file under 'Sa' not 'St'.
- *Figures*: The 2001 Hardware Company: file under 'Two' as though you were saying it.
- De'Ath and similar names: file as if Death, Vansickle, Oleary etc.
- *Nothing comes before something*, e.g. Brown before Browne.
- *Mac, Mc, M' or Mack*: file under 'MAC'.
- *Groups of initials*: keep in a group and file accordingly, e.g. KDA under 'KD'; DHSS under 'DH' etc.
- *Company and personal names*: use the company name, e.g. Charles Lucking trading as BPA, file under 'BPA'.

If in doubt, check in The Phone Book for guidance.

1.3.3 Keeping track

Keep track of files for which you are responsible, whether they are your files or in transit through you. Try to make sure that all files pass through your hands or are not removed or returned without your knowledge.

- Set up a file loan system, so you know where files have gone;
- Put 'flags' in drawers and other storage equipment to show a file is out;
- Have a set place for files going out, files coming in and files being worked on;
- Keep your indexes up-to-date.

A useful memo to type, photocopy and complete each time a file is removed could contain the following information:

- File name (+reference if any)
- Date taken
- By whom taken
- To be returned by (date)

Keep a copy of this memo in the hanging file, and possibly in the 'Bring Forward' file *(See 1.3.7)* as well.

1.3.4 Weeding/housekeeping

Have a regular 'weed' of redundant files and information: it is a useful job to do when your manager is away, or when moving offices.

1.3 Filing

Stick to any 'expiry' dates: e.g. some information can be destroyed after 3 months, some after 2 years and some must never be destroyed.

'Housekeeping' is particularly important on computer files: disks get cluttered with unnecessary information unless they are *regularly* checked, and redundant files (drafts, re-writes etc.) are deleted.

1.3.5 Electronic filing

Electronic filing is only a different *method* of filing. The principles of filing are the same, but even more important because you cannot immediately see what is on a disk. The following hints might help:

- Give documents meaningful names (not just initials);
- Label disks correctly and with sufficient information;
- Keep disks in proper storage media, duly labelled;
- Keep backup and security disks in different locations *(See 1.11)*;
- Devise and keep an indexing system so other people can find the documents;
- Write disk and document names, or other references, on rough printouts if this is not done automatically.

1.3.6 Systematic filing

Expert filing is a great aid to general office efficiency.

- File regularly (every day, or as and when files are used).
- Keep a 'day' file if necessary: this is an extra copy for yourself of all important correspondence done that day. Concertina files are good for housing these.
- Try not to file under 'Miscellaneous'. You may never find it again!

1.3.7 Bring forward system

A bring forward system helps to make sure that jobs to be done on a certain day in the future are in fact carried out. Concertina files are good for this.

- Allocate a slot per day for two or three weeks hence.
- File a note or document copy in the slot for the day when the job is to be done.
- Check the file daily to see if any jobs are to be done that day or the next.
- At the end of a week, remove the current week's papers and add a new week to the 'front' end of the file.
- Alternatively label your concertina file 1–31 for the days of the month.

Make special notes in your diary as well of jobs to be done in the future.

1.4   Flexitime

1.4.1   Core time
Flexitime is a system where the working hours are slightly flexible. Employees work an agreed *core time*, when they must be at work – say 1000–1600 hours.

1.4.2   Flexitime
Outside the core time, employees can start early and finish at 1600 hours, or start at 1000 hours and finish late, according to their own preference and the convenience of the department or section. For a secretary it is sometimes useful to get in early in the morning to get a quiet start to the day. On the other hand, with correspondence to be signed at the end of the day, it is sometimes better to start and finish later.

Working through lunch times and tea breaks (if any) can be counted as flexitime by agreement.

Any flexitime worked over and above the contracted working hours can be added up to earn flexidays – extra days off.

1.4.3   Records
People working flexitime normally have to complete a weekly sheet stating their actual starting and finishing times, morning and afternoon. The hours worked are then added up, and accrued flexidays off can be taken as agreed.

The record form normally allows for adjustments to the net hours worked for such things as paid overtime, attendance at courses, sickness and any other authorised absence or extra hours.

1.5 Holidays, absences and records

People are away from work, or work odd hours, for a variety of reasons. If you are in charge of attendance/holiday records, or for your own satisfaction, it is important to keep the reasons for absence distinct.

1.5.1 Annual holiday

- This is usually worked out as days per calendar year. The company 'holiday year' may or may not start on 1 January – you will need to check.
- There are often rules about when holidays may and may not be taken. Again, check with the organisation.
- Record such absence as Annual Holiday, or Annual Leave.

1.5.2 Statutory holidays
These are days which almost everyone has off, like Bank Holidays, New Year's Day etc. If the company is totally shut, there is no need to record these days.

1.5.3 Flexidays
Flexidays which have been 'earned' should be recorded separately when they are taken. Record as 'Flexi' *(See 1.4)*.

1.5.4 Compassionate leave/family sickness
Most organisations allow days off for family bereavement and emergency family sickness, without deductions from pay. Some organisations lay down how many days an employee can take in specific circumstances, e.g. 5 days for the death of a parent.

1.5.5 Special days
Some organisations have 'special days', e.g. for Christmas shopping. If the whole company is closed down there is no need to record the day. If special days are taken on an individual basis, these should be recorded separately.

1.5.6 Sickness

– Absence because of ill health should be recorded separately, particularly because of SSP (Statutory Sick Pay) *(See 5.3.6)*. There will be company rules to follow about notification of absence through ill health and SSP forms to sign. If in doubt, ask the local DHSS office – ask for Freefone DHSS *(See section on Telephone Services 3.16)*.

– Many organisations run a Sick Pay Scheme, allowing employees a sliding scale of pay according to the length of absence. Accurate recording of absence through illness is equally important on this front.

1.5.7 Unauthorised absence

Absence for no 'good' reason is often penalised by loss of pay. Check the company rules and keep strict records. This is very important for disciplinary reasons.

1.5.8 Shift work and overtime

– It is sometimes the secretary's job to record when people are in and out on shift work. (Shift work is not the same as flexitime, because shift work hours are not normally flexible.)

– Accurate recording of shift work, whether by 'signing in' or by clock card, is vital for the calculation of correct pay.

– The same applies to overtime, for which extra is normally paid.

1.5.9 Time off in lieu

People are sometimes given 'time off in lieu' (i.e. instead of pay) for overtime or some special hours they have worked. Record this separately: it does not come under any of the headings given above.

1.6 Photocopying tips

Check the programming is right before you start copying – the person before you may have left it on A3 when you want A4 copies.

If you have a lot of copies to make, copy just one and check it before setting the counter to the right number.

If you start with the last page the documents will be in the right order as they come out of the photocopier.

It is best to remove paper clips and staples from documents before copying the papers; keeping a stapler and staple remover by the photocopier can be useful.

It is also useful to have the name of the person responsible for the photocopier visible by it, perhaps with a fault record book, so that if it breaks down it gets reported as soon as possible.

Find out how to top up the toner or fluids and to clear paper that is jammed – it is quicker to do these simple things yourself.

If the words on the document to be copied go right to the edge of the paper you could try reducing it to 99% to give a border to the text.

When copying a document with writing on both sides of the paper, e.g. a newspaper cutting, to prevent the writing on the wrong side from coming through you could adjust the exposure control to make the copy lighter and then take a copy of the copy (not of the original) with the exposure control adjusted to darker.

The 2-page separator can be used for doing two single A4 sheets more quickly. *(See 3.10.1)*

Although modern photocopiers can reproduce colour originals, pencil and blue ink do not come out well on the older models.

Some colours of paper, e.g. pink, may produce a grey background on the copy.

When copying on to coloured paper it is best to change the whole tray of paper, both when starting and finishing, so that different coloured papers do not get mixed together.

If you have used correction fluid on a document you want to photocopy it is best to check that it has dried before starting to copy.

When a section has been stuck on to a sheet of paper there is sometimes a line around the insert on the copy. This can be avoided by using correction fluid around the edges of the insert.

Transparencies can be very useful for superimposing designs on text as the text is copied.

A photocopier should not stand right next to a wall. There should be adequate ventilation around it.

1.7 Priorities

Time management and getting the priorities right are essentials for efficient working. Situations vary, but see if this sequence fits yours for a daily routine:

Oman*	968	Surinam*	597
Pakistan	92	Swaziland*	268
Panama	507	Sweden	46
Papua New		Switzerland	41
Guinea*	675	Syria	963
Paraguay	595	Taiwan	886
Peru	51	Tanzania	255
Philippines	63	Thailand	66
Poland	48	Togo*	228
Portugal	351	Tonga*	676
Puerto Rico	1 809	Trinidad and	
		Tobago*	1 809
Qatar*	974	Tunisia	216
Reunion*	262	Turkey	90
Romania	40	Turks and	
St Kitts and		Caicos Islands*	1 809 946
Nevis*	1 809 465	Uganda	256
St Lucia*	1 809 45	United Arab	
St Pierre and		Emirates	971
Miquelon	508	Uruguay	598
St Vincent and		USA	1
the Grenadines	1 809 45	USSR	7
Samoa (US)*	684		
Samoa (Western)*	685	Vanuatu*	678
San Marino*	39 541	Vatican City	
Saudi Arabia	966	State	39 66982
Senegal*	221	Venezuela	58
Seychelles*	248	Virgin Islands	1 809 49
Sierra Leone	232	Yemen Arab	
Singapore*	65	Republic	967
Solomon Islands*	677	Yugoslavia	38
Somalia	252		
South Africa	27	Zaire	243
Spain	34	Zambia	260
Sri Lanka	94	Zimbabwe	263
Sudan	249		

1.9.3 Receiving calls

- Always have a notepad handy.
- Identify yourself clearly and pleasantly; make sure you are speaking directly into the mouthpiece so that your first words are not lost.
- Make sure you know to whom you are speaking.
- Listen to what the caller wants.

–Give information, take messages or
make arrangements as required.
–Check names, addresses and figures
of any sort.
–Agree the action, if any, each of you
is to take.

1.9 Telephone
techniques

–Never be rude.
–Use the caller's name.
–Concentrate on the call – do not be distracted.
–Complete the call in a definite manner.

1.9.4 Making calls

–Always have a notepad handy.
–Make a note of the main things you want to say, and any
references which will help.
–Make sure you are speaking to the right person.
–Identify yourself clearly.
–Put your points or questions clearly and concisely.
–Listen.
–Say what you want the person on the other end to do.
–Check what action (if any) each of you is to take; check
particularly names, addresses and figures of any kind.
–Never be rude.
–Complete the call in a definite manner.

1.9.5 Leaving messages on an answering machine

–If you have to leave a message on an answering machine, the
notes you have made about what you want to say will be a great
help.
–State not only your name, telephone number and the subject of
your call, but remember to say
(*a*) the date *and time* of your call (it helps the owner of the
answering machine when messages are played back, perhaps
from a distance (*See* **3.1**));
(*b*) what you want the receiver of the call to do, e.g. ring back or
wait for you to call again.
–Make sure names, addresses and telephone numbers are very
clear – repeat them if necessary. It is frustrating for the receiver
not to be able to respond to the call.

1.9.6 Using 'new' facilities (See 3.16)

In general, a linked internal system of telephone facilities makes life easier, but there are some extra courtesies necessary to maintain good telephone working relations. *Keep your caller or receiver informed of what you are doing.*

- If you are putting a caller on automatic hold, say so.
- If you are using music on hold, make sure it is played at the right speed.
- If you are switching to loud-speaker mode, so that the conversation goes all round the office, say so.
- When using loud-speaker mode, make sure the mike is not covered.
- If someone else in your office is listening and might be joining in the conversation, say so.
- Use the mute button with discretion. As a caller, it is disconcerting suddenly to find the receiver's voice has disappeared – you tend to think you have been cut off.
- If your line gets disconnected, the original caller should call again.
- Do not hang on for too long if an extension is engaged; ask for the person you are calling to ring back – it saves the company money.

1.10 Typing tips

Always correct carbon or photocopies when the top copy has been altered, so that you have a true record.

Follow house style for layouts of letters, memos, minutes, reports and other common documents *(See Unit 2)*.

Keep copies of useful layouts etc. in a personal file for reference.

Follow house style for forms of address, e.g. whether or not senders and recipients of memos *(See 2.9)* should have titles (Esq, Mr, Mrs, Miss, Ms etc.). Some companies give:

- titles to women but not to men;
- titles to recipients but not to senders;
- initials and surnames only;
- forenames and surnames only.

Open flaps on thick envelopes before winding into the typewriter or printer.

Check tabs are correctly set, or printing point is in the right place for corrections, by setting typewriter on stencil and doing a dummy run (this is less likely to be possible on modern machines).

Do not use correcting fluid which is too thick; thin it or throw it away.

1.11 Word processing tips

For a fuller description of word processing principles, disk management etc., see *Teach Yourself Word Processing*, published by Hodder and Stoughton.

Devise and keep to a system for naming files (documents) and make document names meaningful.

Devise and keep an indexing system for cataloguing file names.

Store disks in correct holders, properly labelled.

On long documents, print out rough copy on scrap paper, with fabric ribbon, and mark disk name, document name, page number and printing details for future reference.

If a document runs onto several disks, use the same document name on each disk; it makes transfer of information easier.

Use carbon ribbons for top copy, fabric for drafts and rough printouts.

Listen to the printer (except laser printers); if the sound is not right, check the printout.

Keep security copies of important documents in a fire-proof and smoke-proof safe, preferably in another part of the building.

Keep a backup copy of your system or software disk, and use it *only* for initialising disks and checking whether your everyday software disk has become corrupted.

Take regular backup copies of incomplete work and work which will need revision.

When using thick envelopes in the printer, open the flap of the envelope and hold the bail bar (if there is one) down as the address is being printed out; the pressure helps provide grip between the envelope and the platen.

When using labels, use a strip of labels and not one or two – it saves them getting wound round the platen.

2.1 Abbreviations (including weights and measures)

(For abbreviations used in addressing letters abroad see 2.3.1.)
(For banking abbreviations see 7.2.3.)
(For abbreviations of professional and academic qualifications see 2.4.2.)

a/c	account	cif	cost, insurance and freight
ack	acknowledged		
AD	after Christ (Anno Domini)	Cllr	Councillor
		cm	centimetre
ad lib	at pleasure (ad libitum)	c/o	cash order; care of; carried over
aka	also known as	COD	cash/collect on delivery
AOB	any other business		
appx	appendix	coh	cash on hand
APR	Annual Percentage Rate	Comr	Commissioner
		contd	continued
asap	as soon as possible	Corpn	Corporation
		cp	compare
av	average	cpd	compound
ave	average	cum	cumulative
Ave	Avenue	CV	Curriculum Vitae (pl: Curricula Vitae)
BC	before Christ		
bc	blind copies		
B/F, b/f	bring forward; brought forward	cwt	hundredweight
b/o	brought over	dsp	died without issue (decessit sine prole)
B/R, b rec	bills receivable		
B/S	balance sheet; bill of sale	DV	God willing (Deo Volente)
c	approximately, circa	E	estimated
cc	copies	e & oe	errors and omissions excepted
c & d	collection and delivery	eg	for example (exempli gratia)
cd	carried down		
cd fwd, c/f, cf	carried forward	enc(l)(s)	enclosure(s)
c & f	cost and freight	et al	and others (et alii/alia)
cf	compare		
chq	cheque	etc	et cetera

ex off	by virtue of one's office (ex officio)
fax	facsimile
ff	following
ffy, ffly	faithfully
fob	free on board
foc	free of carriage
ft	foot, feet
g	gramme(s)
GDP	gross domestic product
GMT	Greenwich mean/meridian time
GNP	gross national product
GP	General Practitioner
grm	gramme(s)
gsm	grammes per square metre
gr wt	gross weight
HRH	Her/His Royal Highness
hrs	hours
id	the same
ie	that is (id est)
Inc	Incorporated
inc(l)	including
inst	of the current month
int al	among others (inter alia)
JP	Justice of the Peace
kg, kilo	kilogramme(s)
kl	kilolitre
km	kilometre
l	litre
lc	lower case
loc	letter of credit
Ltd	Limited
m	metre; mile
max	maximum
memo	memorandum (pl: memoranda)
mg	milligramme(s)

Mgr	Monseigneur
mgr	manager
misc	miscellaneous
ml	millilitre(s)
MP	Member of Parliament
mpg	miles per gallon
mph, m/h	miles per hour
MS	manuscript
msc	miscellaneous
msc	moved, seconded and carried
N/A	no advice; not applicable
NB	take note, remember (nota bene)
nd	not dated
necy	necessary
nem con, nem dis	no one against
nis	not in stock
nmc	no more credit
np	new paragraph
ob	deceased (obiit)
O/D	on demand; overdraft, overdrawn
OHP	overhead projector
oka	otherwise known as
o/o/o	out of order
oos	out of stock
osp	died without issue (obiit sine prole)
oz	ounce(s)
p	page
P & L	Profit and Loss

These could be omitted if they will be different for each application or there is some other reason.

In setting out *qualifications* gained these details may be relevant:
- title of qualification
- when it was gained
- where it was gained
- the grade awarded

Under this heading you might also want to mention any training courses you have attended, even if no certificate was awarded for the course.

In the *work experience* section these are the details you may want to include:

- name and address of employer
- type of business
- job title
- brief details about the work if the job title is not self-explanatory
- whether part-time or full-time
- salary
- starting and leaving dates
- the reason for leaving

As a CV is usually only updated from time to time, and therefore not specifically geared to any particular job, it is usually a good idea to write a covering letter.

The purpose of a covering letter is to state why you want the job and why you think you would be suitable for it. In this letter you can bring out the points from your CV that are relevant to the particular job. For example, on your CV it may say that you were a junior secretary for 12 months, but you might not have space to say that you stood in for the senior secretary for some time. You could mention that in the covering letter.

It is a good idea to keep a copy of the CV, preferably the original, from which to make further copies unless it is stored on disk.

2.3   Foreign words and phrases

ab initio	from the beginning
addendum	something to be added (pl: addenda)
ad hoc	for this special occasion
ad infinitum	to infinity

a fortiori	all the more
alias	otherwise known as
ante	before, preceding (prefix)
anti	against (prefix)
a posteriori	reasoning from effect to cause
a priori	reasoning from cause to effect
ceteris paribus	other things being equal
cave	beware
caveat	let him/her beware
caveat emptor	let the buyer beware
de facto	in reality, as a matter of fact
de novo	again, afresh
ergo	therefore
erratum	error (pl: errata)
et alia/alii	and others (things/people)
ex gratia	free, as a favour
gratis	free
ibid	in the same place/book
in absentia	in his/her absence
in camera	in private (usually applied to legal proceedings)
inter alia	among other things
loc(o) cit(ato)	in the place cited above
nom de plume	literary pseudonym
non sequitur	something that is not a logical consequence
op(ere) cit(ato)	work cited above
pace . . .	by leave of . . . (ironic apology)
per annum	yearly
per capita	per person
per diem	daily
per se	in itself
post	after, following
post mortem	after death
prima facie	on the face of it, at first sight
primo	firstly
pros and cons	in favour of and against
pro forma	as a matter of form; any standard form
pro rata	in proportion
quid pro quo	tit for tat

secundo	secondly
sine die	no date has yet been set
stet	let it stand, leave it as it is
sub judice	in the process of being heard by a court
subpoena	a writ demanding a person's presence in court
supra	above
ultimo	last
ultra vires	outside the powers
verbatim	word for word
vis-à-vis	with regard to
videlicet	namely

2.3.1   Addressing a letter abroad

English	French	German	Spanish	Italian
Mr	M	Herr	Sñr	Sr
Miss	Mlle	Fräulein	Sñrta	Srina
Mrs	Mme	Frau	Sñra	Sra
Messrs	MM	Firma	Sres	Spett. Ditta
c/o	chez	bei	supplicada en casa de	presso
Ltd	S.A.	GmbH	S.A.	Società anonima
Co.	Co	Komp.	Cía	Co

Note: "Ms" has no equivalent in these languages.

2.4   Forms of address and professional qualifications

2.4.1   Forms of address
Below are listed the forms of address you are more likely to need. For each position only the formal way of opening a letter and the way of addressing the envelope are given. For any positions not included here, or for how to open social letters and address the person when speaking to him or her, see a reference book on the subject such as *Debrett's Correct Form* (published by Debretts, and in paperback by Futura Publications) or *Titles and Forms of Address – A Guide to Correct Use* (published by Black).

Anglican clergy
Archbishop
Envelope: The Most Reverend and Rt Hon the Lord Archbishop of Canterbury/York

Opening: My Lord Archbishop,
         Your Grace
Bishop
Envelope: The Right Reverend the
          Lord Bishop of . . .
Opening: My Lord (Bishop)
Vicar/Rector
Envelope: The Reverend John Pike;
          The Reverend J Pike
Opening: Reverend Sir; Dear Sir

Roman Catholic clergy
Archbishop
Envelope: His Grace the Archbishop of . . . or
          The Most Reverend James Smith, Archbishop of . . .
Opening: My Lord Archbishop, Your Grace
Bishop
Envelope: The right Reverend John Dunne, Bishop of . . .
Opening: My Lord (Bishop)
Monsignor
Envelope: The Reverend Mgr Bruce Cheshire, or The Reverend
          Monsignore
Opening: Reverend Sir
Priest
Envelope: The Reverend Father Joseph Greene
Opening: Dear Reverend Father

Politicians
Cabinet Ministers
Envelope: The Secretary of State for . . .
Opening: Dear Sir/Madam
Ministers
Envelope: James Brown Esq MP
Opening: Dear Minister
Ordinary MPs
Envelope: James Brown Esq MP
Opening: Dear Mr Brown

Judiciary
High Court Judges
Envelope: The Hon Mr Justice Roger, The Hon Mrs Justice
          James
if titled: The Hon Sir Mark Roger, The Hon Dame Joy James
Opening: My Lord/Lady, Sir/Madam

2.5.3   Infinitives

An infinitive is a verb in the 'to . . .' form, such as 'to go', 'to type'.
You should try not to split the infinitive up by putting another word
in the middle, e.g.
   'To boldly go . . .'
This is better written as:
   'to go boldly . . .'
   (In some cases 'Boldly to go . . .' might sound better.)
Splitting an infinitive may be acceptable if the sentence would
otherwise sound very stilted or be ambiguous.

2.5.4   Prepositions, e.g. 'to', 'with', 'from', 'up'.

In formal writing it is better not to end sentences with a preposition,
e.g.
   'This is the threat we are faced *with*.'
In a formal context this should be changed to:
   'This is the threat *with which* we are faced.'
The same point applies to clauses. A clause is a group of words
within a sentence which contains a verb with a subject, e.g.
   'The person *you are writing to* is well known to me.'
The main words in the sentence are 'The person . . . is well known
to me.' and they make sense on their own. The clause is the group of
words which will *not* make a complete sentence on its own: 'you are
writing to' ('are writing' is the verb and 'you' is the subject).

   You can see that this clause 'you are writing to' ends with the
preposition 'to'. In a formal context this could be changed to: 'to
whom you are writing'. The sentence would then read:
   'The person to whom you are writing is known to me.'

2.5.5   Singular/plural

If a subject is singular then its verb should be singular as well.

   A verb is a word of action, such as 'go', 'working'. The subject is
the person or thing who is doing the action, e.g.
   'The minister has resigned from office.'
In this sentence 'has resigned' is the verb and 'the minister' is the
subject of that verb.
The difficulty lies in deciding if a subject is singular or plural, e.g.

   'The train' is obviously singular – there is only one train.
   'The ticket collectors' is obviously a plural subject – there is more
   than one ticket collector.

'Each' goes with a verb in the singular, e.g.
   'Each of our departments *is* well stocked.'

'Either' and 'neither': if both subjects are singular then so is the verb, e.g.

'*Neither* the train *nor* the coach *stops* there.'

If both subjects are plural then so is the verb, e.g.

'*Either* bottles *or* glasses *are* available.'

But if one subject is singular and one is plural then the verb should agree with the subject just before it, preferably the plural one, e.g.

'*Either* cash *or* credit cards *are* accepted.'

'Less/fewer': generally speaking 'less' is used with a singular subject and 'fewer' with a plural subject, e.g.

'We'll need *less paper* and *fewer pens* this time because there will be *fewer people*.'

The verb must correspond too, e.g.

'Less paper *is* needed.'

'Fewer people *are* coming.'

'None': like 'either' and 'neither', whether the verb following 'none' is singular or plural depends on the subject. If the subject is singular the verb will be singular, e.g.

'None of the food *was* edible.'

If the subject is plural the verb may be either singular or plural, e.g.

'None of the glasses *is* clean.'

'None of the cats *are* friendly.'

If you use the singular verb you are emphasising the fact that every single glass was dirty. In the example of the cats the impression is more of a group of hostile animals than of considering each one individually.

'Public' etc: you will find words referring to a collection of people used with both singular and plural verbs according to the taste of the writer. This includes words such as 'group', 'company', 'government' and 'committee'.

2.6 Invitations and forms of dress

2.6.1 *Formal invitations*

These are written and answered in the third person.

An example invitation is shown overleaf

The Chairman and Directors
request the pleasure of the company of
Mr Rohan Saxena
at Greenwood Lodge
on Saturday 11th December 198–
at 8 pm

Black tie   RSVP

Example reply

Mr Rohan Saxena
accepts with pleasure
the kind invitation of
The Chairman and Directors
for Saturday 11th December

Neither the invitation nor the reply is signed. 'Carriages' and a time at the bottom of an invitation indicate at what time it is expected to end.

Less formal invitations can be written in the form of an ordinary business letter (or a memo if internal). See example opposite.

2.6.2   Forms of dress

'White tie':   Full evening dress i.e. black tails and trousers with a white bow tie for men; floor-length clothes for women.

'Black tie':   Dinner jacket, black trousers and black bow tie for men; formal but not necessarily floor-length clothes for women.

'Lounge suit': Smart business dress.

2.7   Letters

2.7.1   General layout

The simplest thing to do is to follow the house style as to the layout of letters. Going down the page, the order in which the different parts come is usually something like this:

1   sender's address
2   sender's telephone number
3   reference
4   date
5   addressee's title (or name) and address
6   salutation (opening)

2.6	Invitations and forms of dress
2.7	Letters

Example:

OTT Promotions Ltd
15 Main Street
COVENTRY
Warwickshire CV1 7RE

The Editor
Coventry Weekly
13 Main Street
COVENTRY
Warwickshire
CV1 7RD

25th August 198-

Our Ref: MF/SG

Dear Mrs Lambert

Press Conference: 9th September 198-

You are invited to attend a Press Conference given by OTT Promotions Ltd to release their Annual Report and announce their revised approach to marketing tactics in the light of the recent Government White Paper.

The Conference will be held at the above address on Friday 9th September beginning at 12.00 noon. There will be a buffet lunch to follow.

It would be greatly appreciated if you would contact Sheila Grey on extension 219 to indicate whether or not you (or a colleague) will be able to attend.

Yours sincerely

Mary Friel (Miss)
Public Relations Officer

7   blocked or centred heading
8   body of the letter
9   complimentary close (sometimes called subscription)
10 signature
11 enclosures
12 copies

Numbers 1 and 2 are usually typed on the righthand side of the page when there is no official letterhead.

If it is up to you which style to adopt then the choice is between *blocked*, *semi-blocked* and *indented*. *(For examples of the blocked and semi-blocked styles see 2.7.12.)* The indented style is rarely used. An indented address is one where each line of the address starts further in than the one before it:

102 Broad Street
    Midtown
        Wessex
            WX1 1AA

A *blocked* address is one where all the lines are aligned to the left margin. This is quicker to type than an indented address. A *fully blocked* letter is one where all the lines are aligned to the left margin except for numbers 1 and 2 above.

A *semi-blocked* letter is a mixture of styles. The addresses may not be indented while the paragraphs are. Alternatively, the heading may be centred and the subscription may be typed to the right from the centre of the letter. (The salutation is never centred.)

2.7.2   Punctuation

As above, if there is a house style then it is best to follow that. The body of the letter is always punctuated. The salutation and subscription may have a comma at the end or may not. Similarly the addresses may be fully punctuated (comma at the end of each line and full stop before the postcode) or not, according to taste. However, if you decide to put commas at the end of the salutation and the subscription but not to punctuate the addresses or date etc, there should not be any full stops after 'Mr' or 'Mrs'. (As 'Ms' is not really an abbreviation of a longer word a full stop after it is not essential, but practice varies.) The punctuation of titles should be consistent throughout the whole letter (and envelope).

2.7.3   Reference

If the letter in hand is in reply to one with a reference it should always be quoted. It usually goes on the lefthand side of the page beneath the address. If it is more than just the initials of those responsible for sending the letter it could be put as the centre heading – it will stand out more.

2.7 Letters

2.7.4 Salutation

If you know the name of the addressee then you can open the letter using the name rather than the job title. It is courteous to use the title which the addressee prefers. If the letter is addressed to a woman and you are unsure whether she uses 'Miss', 'Mrs' or 'Ms' it is good business practice to try and find out, by looking at past correspondence or by ringing her secretary. ('Ms' is the equivalent of 'Mr' in that it does not indicate whether a woman is married.)

In some businesses it is becoming acceptable to use the addressee's first name and surname, e.g. 'Dear Jill Northend', particularly if the title is unknown.

If the letter is to a firm whose name begins 'Messrs . . .' then the salutation should read 'Dear Sirs' as it is to the firm, not any one individual. The address would then be headed 'For the attention of . . .' (F.A.O. . . .) both on the letter and the envelope.

2.7.5 Heading

It is often a good idea to put a heading so that the recipient can see immediately what the letter is about. It should be underlined and may or may not be centred.

2.7.6 Complimentary close

This may be centred, blocked or typed from the middle of the line of writing. If a person's name is used in the salutation the letter is closed with 'Yours sincerely'. If the letter is to 'Dear Madam', 'Dear Sir' or 'Dear Sirs' the subscription is 'Yours faithfully'.

2.7.7 Signature

This follows the subscription, i.e. if the subscription is centred then so will the signature be. Six carriage returns is usually enough space for a signature. After that the sender's name is typed with the title before or after the name in brackets if necessary and the job title underneath.

If the person actually signing the letter is not the one whose name appears at the bottom of the letter then 'pp' or 'per pro' should be written in front of that typed name. (This is an abbreviation of the Latin term 'per procurationem' and means 'for and on behalf of'.)

2.7.8 Enclosures
If anything is sent with the letter this should be indicated by 'enc(s)' below the sender's name. This alerts the addressee to check that the enclosure arrived and is kept with the letter.

2.7.9 Copies
If copies of the letter are sent to people other than the addressee then this should be indicated by the letters 'cc' and the names of those other people. Because 'cc' stands for 'carbon copy' and carbon copies are infrequently used, some people type 'Copy to'.

2.7.10 Blind copies
This is where a copy is sent to someone who is not the addressee but it is not indicated on the letter. For example, the manuscript may have
    cc Rachel O'Dowd
    bc Charles Walker
at the bottom. This tells the secretary to send Rachel O'Dowd a copy as normal and to show this on the letter, but also to send a copy to Charles Walker without putting his name at the bottom of the letter.

2.7.11 Envelope
The address on the envelope should be in the same style as that in the letter. If the letter is personal or confidential this should be typed on the envelope (usually in capitals).

2.7.12 Examples of blocked and semi-blocked layouts

Fully blocked

```
                                        Trekkers Ltd
                                        59 Catherine St
                                        OXFORD
                                        OX3 5RA

                                        (0865) 12345
Your Ref: CD/10/HS

Our Ref: RL/JB

9 December 198-

Miss C Danby
Public Relations Manager
R C L Ltd
139 Main St
MIDTOWN
Wessex
WX1 1RB

Dear Miss Danby

[Heading]

[Body of the letter.]

[Punctuated normally and all paragraphs aligned to the left
hand margin.]

Yours sincerely



R E Lambert (Ms)

cc   R Weller
```

Semi-blocked

Trekkers Ltd.,
59 Catherine St.,
OXFORD.
OX3 5RA

(0865) 12345

Your Ref: CD/10/HS

Our Ref: RL/JB

9 December 198–

Miss C. Danby
Public Relations Manager,
R.C.L. Ltd.,
139 Main St.,
MIDTOWN,
Wessex.
WX1 1AA

Dear Miss Danby,

[*Heading*]

[Body of the letter.]

[The first line of each paragraph is indented five characters – easily done with the tab key.]

Yours sincerely

R.E. Lambert (Ms)

cc   R. Weller

2.8   Mail and mailroom equipment

For Electronic mail see 3.5.

2.8.1   Incoming mail

- Sort the mail into 'Private', envelopes and parcels as appropriate.
- Check enclosures have been enclosed. Attach them to the accompanying letter.

—In the case of parcels, check the packing note or invoice against the contents and that the contents are undamaged.
—Check that remittances tally with the amount stated in the letter or Remittance Advice *(see 10.17)*.

—You may wish to attach the relevant file to the correspondence before delivering it.
—Note the date of arrival – either in the post book or on the letter.
—Distribute the mail.

2.8.2 Outgoing mail

—Check that each letter has been signed and has the relevant enclosures attached.
—Enter the date of sending in the post book, if appropriate.
—Divide into special mail, parcels and ordinary mail. The Post Office provides leaflets on how to wrap parcels and valuable items.
—Divide the ordinary mail into 1st and 2nd class.
—Weigh and stamp all letters – check that you are using an up-to-date leaflet on the postal rates.
—Face the letters, that is, make sure they are all the same way up and facing the same way.
—Keep the 1st and 2nd class separate. If the post is to be handed in at a London Post Office then separate the mail for London addresses from mail for other parts of the country.
—Record the postage following company practice.
—Prepare a certificate of posting for any Recorded Delivery mail (certificates available from Post Offices).

Note that if a business sends a certain minimum of letters or parcels per day then the Post Office will collect them free of charge.

2.8.3 Mailroom equipment
It is self-evident from the names of most of these machines what their function is.

—Addressing machines
—Collators
—Folding machines

- Franking machines: these may be used by special arrangement with the Post Office. For a list of companies authorised to supply them see the *Post Office Guide*. Postage is paid for in advance when a franking machine is used. A weekly record card must be filled in to show the value of postage franked every week, even if the machine has not been used.
- Inserters: these collate, fold and insert documents into envelopes and then seal and stack them.
- Joggers: these shuffle large stacks of documents into neat piles. They are used for large mailings.
- Openers
- Scales
- Sealers
- Sponge-dampers: for sealing envelopes without licking them.
- Tying machines

A secretary who handles the mail will most likely need scales, a franking machine and a sponge-damper. The other machines are more likely to be found in company mailrooms.

2.9   Memoranda

Memos are internal documents. They may be very formal and always typed on specially headed paper, or they may be little more than a typed-up note.

A5 landscape paper is suitable for short memos. If you use a word processor then you may want to design your own form memo. Then each time you only have to call up the form, key in the headings and the text, and print the whole thing out on plain paper.

Memos are not usually signed, although the sender's name should be typed on the memo. However, if financial transactions are involved some businesses initial or sign memos.

Memos may be addressed to people according to their job title,

e.g. To: Personnel Manager.

Alternatively, they may be addressed using a title (Mr, Mrs, Miss, Ms etc.), first names and surnames or initials and surnames. The easiest thing to do is to follow the house style.

For the layout of a memo, again it is best to follow the house style if there is one. If there is no house style then you can design your own layout, including the details shown on the following page below the Box.

It is always useful to the person receiving a memo to include a heading so the subject of the memo can be seen at a glance.

As with letters, enclosures and copies are indicated at the bottom of the memo by the abbreviations 'Enc(s)' and 'cc' (or 'copies to'). Also as for letters, a copy should be kept of all memos sent out.

To	Date
From	Ref
Subject	

2.10 Post Office services

For up-to-date details of Post Office services see the *Post Office Guide* or enquire at any main Post Office.

2.10.1 Inland
Services to Eire, the Channel Islands and the Isle of Man are broadly the same as those for inland services but there are differences so it is best to check.

Business Reply Service This is where a company issues pre-paid cards addressed to itself. The potential client can then return the card without paying any postage. The company pays the charges on all replies received. It is the sort of service which is useful for encouraging customers to request more information, such as a catalogue. Anyone wanting to use this service must obtain a licence from the Post Office.

Cash On Delivery For parcels, packets and 1st class letters. All packets and letters sent COD must be registered. The COD amount is specified by the sender to be collected by the postman on delivery of the package. The amount can then be sent to the sender of the package by the Post Office.

Datapost This is a courier service. Delivery is guaranteed by noon the next day (to most areas) or your money back. Maximum weight 27.5kg per item. This service also operates internationally which obviously takes longer. The maximum weight per item depends on the country to which the package is being sent but is generally 20kg.

Freepost   Items sent under this service will be treated as 2nd class mail only. It is similar to the Business Reply Service. The difference is that the customer will write the company's address, including the word FREEPOST, on the item, rather than using a pre-paid card. A licence must be obtained to use this service.

Intelpost   This is a facsimile service. The fax is handed in at a specified centre and can either be collected from a specified Post Office or will be delivered as normal 1st class mail. There is a same day delivery to specified postal areas.

Newspapers   A publication which is registered as a newspaper with the Post Office is paid for at the 2nd class rate but treated as 1st class mail. Maximum weight 750g. See the *Post Office Guide* for details of what may qualify as a newspaper.

Nightrider   This is an overnight delivery service for the London Postal Region. Parcels must be handed in at a main Post Office. Maximum weight 25kg.

Parcels   Weight limit 25kg.

Postage Forward Parcel Service   This is where the addressee pays the postage. As for the Business Reply Service, a licence must be obtained from the Post Office.

Recorded delivery   This may be used for 1st and 2nd class letters. A letter to be sent recorded delivery must be handed in at a Post Office with the fee payable. The Post Office will record the acceptance of the letter or package at a specified address (but not by a particular person). It is possible to arrange for an advice of delivery to be sent to the sender. It is not a suitable way of sending valuable items.

Registered letters   Only 1st class letters may be sent registered. A certificate of posting must be obtained on handing the letter in at a Post Office. A registration fee is payable in addition to 1st class postage. You can arrange for an advice of delivery to be sent to the sender.

Royal Mail Special Delivery   This is available only for 1st class post. It is a special assurance that the mail will arrive the next working day. A fee is payable in addition to the postage.

2.10.2   International
A Customs Declaration will be needed for anything sent abroad other than letters or printed papers *(See 10.7)*.

Airmail Letters from the UK to Europe are normally sent Airmail. Items sent outside Europe by the Airmail service must have a blue label or the words PAR AVION/BY AIRMAIL written in the top left-hand corner. *See also 'Swiftair' below.*

> **2.10** Post Office services
> **2.11** Punctuation

Cash on Delivery Parcels may be sent abroad for cash on delivery which is called the 'Trade Charge'.

Express delivery Items not acceptable for Swiftair service (see below) may be sent by Express. Such items include parcels and printed papers to Europe, and surface letters and printed papers to countries outside Europe.

Intelpost This service *(see under 2.10.1 Inland services above)* also operates internationally.

Parcels The weight limit is normally 10kg. If the package weighs only 500g or 1kg the letter or small packet services may be cheaper.

Printed Papers Items acceptable for this service may be sent at a reduced rate. Such items include advertisements, books, calendars, catalogues, newspapers and periodicals. They must be unsealed. Correspondence cannot be sent by this service.

Surface Mail Items sent outside Europe may be sent by Airmail *(see above)* or by surface mail. The weight limit for letters is 2kg. There is a special category called 'Small Packets'. The weight limit for this is usually 1kg and such packets may not include any correspondence.

Swiftair This is an express letter service which aims to deliver at least 1 day earlier than ordinary Airmail. The weight limit is 2kg. A Swiftair label must be used. Within Europe the service will take letters, packets and newspapers. Outside Europe you can use this service for airmail letters, printed papers and small packets.

2.11 Punctuation and hyphenation

2.11.1 Punctuation – some common problems

Apostrophe ' *(For 'its/it's', 'who's/whose' and 'they're/their' see 'Confusibles' 2.13.2)*

The apostrophe has two functions: to show possession or to show a word has been contracted or shortened.

Possession   An apostrophe followed by an 's' denotes possession, e.g.

James's school

This may also be written 'James' school' because the word 'James' ends in an 's'.

Note the difference between these two examples:

The girl's books   The girls' books

In the first example the books belong to one girl. In the second example the books belong to more than one girl. As in the example with the word 'James' above, because the word 'girls' ends in an 's' the second 's' which would normally follow the apostrophe is dropped.

Contraction   The apostrophe denotes that one or more letters are missing, e.g.

I'm coming tomorrow.

The apostrophe can also indicate the plural of an abbreviation. Thus: 1980's, MP's, GP's, but you will also see these plurals written without an apostrophe.

If the apostrophe denotes possession, e.g. the MP's secretary, it should never be left out.

Brackets () and full stops .   If a group of words is placed inside a pair of brackets as part of a sentence there can be no full stop inside the brackets e.g.

'It will take 30 mins to reach the town from the motorway exit (exit number 5).'

Where the words in brackets form a complete sentence on their own and are not part of a longer sentence the full stop comes before the 2nd bracket e.g.

'The meeting has been provisionally fixed for 10th April. (I will confirm this date nearer the time.)'

Colons :   A colon makes a break in a sentence where the second half is an illustration or explanation of the first. It can also be used to introduce a list. It has the same effect as if you put 'i.e.':

'Check that these days have been kept free: 7 Jan, 13 Jan, 2 Feb.'

Commas ,   These should not be used to separate two sentences.

'I refer to our telephone conversation of 1st December, I am

writing to confirm the order.'
This should read:

> 'I refer to our telephone conversation of 1st December. I am writing to confirm the order.'

| **2.11** Punctuation |

Commas in lists   Items in lists are usually separated by a comma (although see 'Semicolons' below) except for the last two items which are joined by the word 'and'. A comma before the 'and' is sometimes useful for clarity.

> 'We shall need an overhead projector, name cards, pens, paper, and copies of the report.'

> 'We shall need an overhead projector, pens and paper.'

Pairs of commas   Where a comma is introduced to separate a clause from the main part of the sentence a second comma must be used at the end of the clause when you return to the main sentence. *(For a brief explanation of what a clause is see 2.5.4 'Prepositions'.)*

> 'Venice, which is in Italy, is thought to be a romantic place.'

Dash –   Dashes may be used in pairs like brackets to separate a group of words from the surrounding sentence.

> 'Firm-mindedness – or obstinacy, depending on your point of view – can be a useful quality.'

A single dash provides a pause in a sentence. It may be used where what follows illustrates, comments on or sums up the words in the first part of the sentence.

> 'The conference was not very productive – just as you had warned me.'

Dashes are best used sparingly. In particular, using pairs of dashes and single ones in the same sentence can be very confusing.

Hyphens -   For hyphenation as a means of breaking words in the course of typing see below *(see 2.11.2)*. This paragraph deals with the hyphen as punctuation. The general rule is: use a hyphen if it makes the meaning clear where it might otherwise be unclear, e.g.

> 'to reexamine' is not an easy word to understand immediately.

The sequence of letters 'reex' is unfamiliar. A hyphen makes it clearer: 'to re-examine'. Consider also the following:

> A rolling pin is a pin that is rolling off the table, but a rolling-pin is used for rolling out pastry.

Hyphens are *always* used in the following circumstances:

- –between a prefix and a proper name, e.g. anti-Soviet;
- –in writing out fractions, e.g. three-quarters;
- –where a figure is part of a compound adjective, e.g. four-year delays.

In the last example 'four-year' works as an adjective describing the length of delay. If there were no hyphen 'four year delays' could mean four separate delays of a year each.

Hyphens are *usually* used after the following prefixes: ex, vice, self, and non, e.g. self-awareness, ex-directory.

In the case of other prefixes such as post, co, re, pre, practice varies according to the individual. Thus you will find both 'co-operate and 'cooperate'. The better known a word is the less necessary the hypen will be.

Quoting within a quotation   This means using both double (". . .") and single ('. . .') quotation marks. They should always be used in pairs so it is a matter of making sure they come in the right order. For example: She said, 'I really enjoyed "War and Peace'." is wrong. "War and Peace" is opened by a double quotation mark and should therefore be closed with one (before the full stop). The words she said began with a single quotation mark and therefore close with one (after the full stop). The correct version is this:

She said, 'I really enjoyed "War and Peace".'

Semicolons ;   A semicolon is used to provide a break in a sentence where you do not want to make the second half into a new sentence (by using a full stop) but a comma seems too weak, e.g.

The machine belongs to the purchaser; no licence or rental payment is required.

Semicolons in lists   Another use of a semicolon is in place of commas in a list where commas would not split up the items in the list clearly. This example also shows the difference between a colon and a semicolon. The colon is used to introduce the list and the semicolon is used to break the list into its individual items, e.g.

For Friday's meeting we will need: 6 copies of the report; an OHP if available; name cards stating the person's name and that of the company; pens and paper.

2.11.2   Hyphenation for breaking words
When a word is too long to fit on the end of a line you will want to

break it with a hyphen. Here is a quick guide to when to divide and where.

Never divide:

- a word with only one syllable e.g. mean
- names of people or places
- foreign words
- dates
- sums of money

Where to divide

Type of word	Where to break it
Word already hyphenated	at the hyphen, e.g. anti-American
A compound word	between the two parts of the word, c.g. motor-way
Word starting with a prefix or ending with a suffix	at the prefix or suffix, e.g. pre-requisite, attrac-tion
Words with a double consonant	between the consonants, e.g. occur-rence
Words with 3 consecutive vowels	after the first vowel, e.g. continu-ous
Words with 2 adjacent vowels	between the vowels, e.g. usu-ally
Words which do not fall into any of the categories above	according to the syllables, e.g. sing-ular, import-ant

2.12   Reports

2.12.1   Outline

- Heading
- Reason for the report
- Method
- Findings
- Recommendations/Conclusion

2.12.2   Headings

If a report is long and complicated, a system of headings and sub-headings (using underlining, emboldening, upper and lower case letters) may be useful to make it clearer and to make later references easier. Whichever system you choose, the important thing is to be consistent.

2.12.3   Numbering

A numbering system may be used in conjunction with or instead of a system of headings. Each major section of the report is given a number and the paragraphs are also numbered with a full stop or an oblique in between the two numbers, e.g. 2.5. 12/4.

If there are any lists or sub-divisions within a paragraph lower case letters or small Roman numerals can be used.

2.12.4   Page numbering

This may be unnecessary if you are using a numerical system but will be vital if you are not and the report runs on to three pages or more.

2.12.5   Footnotes

These may go either at the bottom of the relevant page or at the end of the appropriate section. (The latter option is easier if you are not using a word processor.) If there are only a few footnotes to a short report then they can be included at the end of the report itself.

2.12.6   Bibliography

If several sources are referred to in the report, the writer may ask you to include a bibliography. This is a separate list attached to the end of the report of all the books used in the course of researching and writing the report. For each book you should show the title, author, publisher and year of publication.

2.13   Spelling

2.13.1   Mis-spellings

absence	ancillary	benefited	connoisseur
absorption	anonymous	breathe	conscientious
access	anxiety	budgeted	conscious
accessible	apparent	bureau	consistent
accommodation	appearance	bureaucracy	convenience
achievement	appropriate	business	correlate
acknowledge	argument		correspondence
acquaintance	arrangement	category	correspondent
acquiesce	assess	chaos	corroborate
acquisition	assist	colleague	courteous
address	assiduous	commitment	courtesy
aggravate	awful	committed	
agreeable		committee	
amateur	bachelor	compatible	deceive
analysis	beginning	comparative	deficient
(pl. analyses)	believed	competence	definite

dependant
(noun)
dependent
(adjective)
desirable
deterrent
disappear
disappoint
discipline
discreet
discrepancy
dissatisfied
distributor

efficiency
eighth
eliminated
eminent
embarrassment
enthusiasm
equipped
equipment
erroneous
essential
especially
exaggerated
excellent
exercise
exhausted
experience
extremely

favourite
feasible
financial
foreign
forty
fulfil
fulfilled
fulfilment

gauge
government
grievance
guarantee
guard

harassment
height

heroes
honorary
honour
humour
humorous
hypocrisy
hypothesis
(pl: hypotheses)

immediately
immigrant
imminent
incidentally
incipient
independent
indispensable
influential
install
instalment
intelligence
irrelevant
irreparable
irresistible

judg(e)ment
judicial

knowledge

liaison
losing
lying

maintenance
manoeuvre
marriage
Mediterranean

necessary
negotiable
niece
noticeable

occasionally
occur
occurred
occurrence
omit
omitted
omission

parallel
parliament
permanent
permissible
persevere
personnel
persuade
piece
planning
possess
potential
precede
preceding
predecessor
preference
preferred
preliminary
prestige
privilege
procedure
professional
professor
pronunciation
proprietary
psychology
pursue

questionnaire
quiet

received
recommend
referred
reference
relieved
repetition
responsibility

scarcely
seize

sentence
separate
siege
similar
sincerely
skilful
statutory
subtle
subtlety
succeed
successful
successfully
summary
supersede
suppress
surprising
synonym
synonymous

technical
technology
temporary
tendency
transfer
transferred
transference
transient
twelfth

unconscious
underrated
undoubtedly
unfortunately

warehouse
weird
wield
withhold
woollen

yield

2.12 Reports
2.13 Spelling

2.13.2 Confusibles

accept/except 'To accept' is a verb, e.g. 'Yes, I'll accept your offer. 'Except' is a preposition, e.g. 'Everyone's going except me.'

adverse/averse Both these words are adjectives showing a degree of hostility, e.g. 'The launch met an adverse reception; they were averse to the product.' 'Adverse' is stronger than 'averse'. 'Averse' is usually used in the form 'he is averse to . . .'

advice/advise 'Advice' is the noun, e.g. 'Please accept my advice.' 'Advise' is the verb, e.g. 'Please advise me on this problem.'

affect/effect 'Affect' is almost always used as a verb, e.g. 'That wine affected me badly.' 'Effect' can be used as a noun, e.g. 'That wine had a bad effect on me.' It can also be used as a verb when it means to bring something about, e.g. 'To effect a reconciliation' means to make a reconciliation happen.

alternately/alternatively 'Alternately' means 'one after the other', e.g. 'When you walk you use alternate feet.' 'Alternatively' means 'in the alternative' where someone has a choice between two possibilities, e.g. 'You can have soup or, alternatively, you can have a prawn cocktail.'

ante/anti These are both prefixes. 'Ante' means before, as in 'ante-natal'. 'Anti' means against, as in 'anti-smoking'.

censer/censor/censure 'A censer' is an object for holding incense, usually used in churches. 'To censor' is to edit as in the British Board of Film Censors. 'To censure' is to criticise unfavourably or to judge something.

complement/compliment 'To complement' something is to make it complete. 'To compliment' someone is to praise them. Free tickets are complimentary ones.

council/counsel 'A Council' is a noun, as in Local Council of which a member is a Councillor. 'Counsel' may be a verb or a noun. 'To counsel someone' is to give them advice, as does a Marriage Guidance Counsellor. When used as a noun it means advice or, when referring to a person, a barrister.

disinterested/uninterested Someone who is disinterested is acting impartially, not out of self-interest. Someone who is uninterested is bored.

effect/affect *See 'affect' above.*

emigrant/immigrant Which of these words you use to describe someone moving from one country to another depends on your point of view. If that person is leaving the country you are in, she or he will be an emigrant. If she or he is entering the country you are in, he or she is an immigrant.

eminent/imminent An eminent person is an important or famous one. An imminent event is one which is about to happen.

enquire/inquire There is little difference between these two words. 'To enquire' is to ask whereas 'to inquire' is to ask more searchingly. You may enquire about the time of the next train; the police conduct inquiries into crimes.

ensure/insure 'To ensure' is to make sure. To insure something is to take out an insurance policy on it, e.g. 'I have ensured that all my possessions are insured.'

especially/specially *See 'specially' below.*

except/accept *See 'accept' above.*

formally/formerly 'Formally is the opposite of 'informally', whereas 'formerly' means previously.

immigrant/emigrant *See 'emigrant' above.*

imminent/eminent *See 'eminent' above.*

imply/infer 'To imply' something is to convey it without saying it explicitly. 'To infer' something is to deduce it from the given facts.

inquire/enquire *See 'enquire' above.*

insure/ensure *See 'ensure' above.*

it's/its 'It's' means 'it is'. The apostrophe shows the letter 'i' is missing. 'Its' is the equivalent of 'my', 'her', 'their' etc., when applied to a thing, e.g. 'The door's come off its hinge. It's useless now.'

practice/practise 'Practice' is the noun, e.g. 'Some practice would help you improve.' 'Practise' is the verb, e.g. 'You must practise if you want to improve.' The same rule applies as for 'advice' and 'advise'.

precede/proceed 'To precede' is to go before, e.g. 'The meeting will be preceded by lunch.' 'To proceed' is to go ahead, e.g. 'Please proceed with the meeting without me.'

principal/principle Where 'principal' is used as a noun it means the head of something, e.g. of a training college. Where 'principal' is used as an adjective it means 'main', or 'chief', e.g. 'The principal reason for the drop in sales is the difficulty in delivering on time.' 'Principle' is always used as a noun. It means a fundamental belief, e.g. 'I never work on Sundays on principle.'

specially/especially 'Specially' means for a particular purpose, e.g.

'This was made specially for you.' 'Especially' means unusually or to a high degree, e.g. 'This is especially good work.'

stationary/stationery 'Stationary' means unmoving, fixed – it is an adjective. 'Stationery' is a noun referring to pens, paper etc.

storey/story 'Storey' means floor as in 'a five-storey building'. 'Story' means tale as in 'fairy story'.

their/there/they're 'Their' is the equivalent of 'his' or 'her' when referring to more than one person. 'There' is the opposite of 'here'. 'They're' is 'they are' with an apostrophe to show the 'a' is missing.

to/too/two 'To' is used as in 'going to a place'. 'Too' is used to show an excess or for emphasis, e.g. 'Too many cooks spoil the broth.' 'Two' equals 2.

whose/who's 'Whose' is used to show possession of something, e.g. 'The person whose office is on the ground floor . . . Whose office is it?' 'Who's' is the equivalent of 'who is'.

2.14 Visual aids: charts and graphs

The important points to remember when drawing up a graph are the axes and the key. Along each axis must be written what is being measured and what unit of measurement is being used. There should also be a key to show what each type or colour of line represents. For examples see below.

2.14.1 Bar charts (histograms)

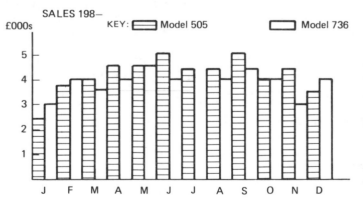

Each block represents an amount of a certain product. The key tells us that the block with horizontal stripes represents Model 505 so, looking at the bar chart it shows that sales of Model 505 were worth £5000 in the month of June.

2.14.2 Line graphs

These are more suitable for demonstrating the progress of any single item over a period of time.

In the example (below) it is easy to see that sales of product A started off well but then dropped over the rest of the year while sales of product B remained fairly steady throughout.

2.13 Spelling
2.14 Visual aids

Again, a key is necessary to distinguish one line from another. You can either draw the lines on or you could use elasticated cord secured with pegs.

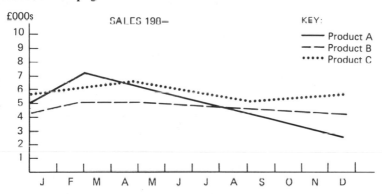

2.14.3 Overhead projector (OHP)

This is essentially the same way of presenting material as using a flip chart *(see 2.15.2)* or black/whiteboard *(see 2.15.3)* but the material is projected from an acetate strip onto a white screen behind the presenter, who can look at the audience. The advantage is that it is easier for the audience to read the material. The presenter can use pre-prepared sheets (transparencies) or write on the sheet (or roll) during the presentation. Special pens are needed to write on the acetate.

There are two problems that sometimes occur when using an OHP:

- the image projected onto the screen may not be rectangular but rather keystone in shape. To correct this you can pull the top of the screen forward until the image is adjusted.
- the lamp may blow in which case the OHP will be useless. In case this happens it is a good idea to have a spare lamp to hand.

2.14.4 Pie charts
These are usually used for showing how a whole figure breaks down into its component elements. The circle is the whole and each segment represents one of the component elements as a percentage of the whole.

For example, the pie chart below represents company expenditure in one financial year. Each segment represents a different area of expenditure as a percentage of the total.

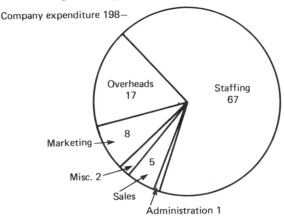

This may also be expressed as so many pence in every pound because there are one hundred pence in every pound. Therefore you can say that the marketing department spent 8% of the total company expenditure, or that 8p in every pound was spent on marketing.

2.14.5 Slide projector
When using a slide projector it is important to put the slides in the correct order before the presentation starts and to number them. If the presenter does not want to stand next to the projector, which usually means standing at the back of the room, a long lead or extension should be made available.

2.15   Visual control boards

2.15.1 Planners
These are available mounted or unmounted. They can be adapted to show specific categories of information. For example, Staff Planners will show the whereabouts of a department of people, and

Year Planners show which days of the year are booked for conferences, holidays etc.

Planners come in a variety of sizes and types. Some can be written on and then wiped clean again. Others are suitable for use only with special indicators, plastic or magnetic. Some have moveable date strips and so can be used for more than one year.

2.14 Visual aids **2.15** Visual control boards

If you are setting up a planner it is best to show the key on the board, e.g. red stripe = holiday.

2.15.2   Flip charts

These usually come on an easel stand. They are available either with pads of paper to be used with ordinary marker pens where the sheets can be fllipped over as they are used, or with re-usable pads of laminated sheets for use with dry-wipe markers. The usual minimum size is A1: 810mm × 585mm ($31\frac{7}{8}''$ × 23″).

2.15.3   Blackboards and whiteboards

Blackboards are slate on which chalk is used. Whiteboards are written on with dry-wipe markers – the writing can then be wiped off. They are also suitable for use as a projection screen.

2.15.4   Statistical charts

These have moveable ribbons which can be extended to the desired length to create a bar chart. If used with pegboards then a linear graph can be created (*see 2.14.2*).

3.1 Answering machines

Answering machines, like telephones, are sold by British Telecom (BT) and other private suppliers. The machine belongs to the purchaser; no licence or rental payment is required.

They are advertised in business/office equipment magazines and sold by business equipment companies and retail outlets which sell standard telephones.

Look for the following features:

- dual cassette for incoming/outgoing messages;
- remote playback (pick up your messages by telephone, using a special bleeper);
- incoming tape cut-off after a certain length of time; it saves people jamming the machine with long, unwanted messages;
- machine incorporated in telephone instrument (telephone and answering machine in one unit).

Connections:
- one into an ordinary power socket;
- one into your telephone system: for new telephone sockets you can buy a two-way adaptor to take the plug from the telephone and the plug from the answering machine; for old sockets you will need an engineer to fit a new socket, or a DIY kit. BT engineers will not normally deal with products sold by other people.

3.2 Care of equipment

Electronic office equipment is not normally sensitive to temperature changes, except great heat (a printer in the sunshine by a window) which could blow a fuse. Therefore temperature-controlled surroundings are not normally necessary.

It is susceptible to dust and dirt: no smoking, drinking or eating should be the rule when using electronic office equipment. Disk drives can be particularly susceptible to smoke.

Follow the rules shown on the following page for care of floppy disks:

DO
- Store them carefully, away from magnetic fields;
- Keep them in their protective envelope when not in use;
- Label them carefully;
- Insert them carefully into the disk drive, without forcing or bending them.

3.1	Answering machines
3.2	Care of equipment
3.3	Computer terminology

DON'T
- Put finger marks on the elongated slot where information is recorded and read;
- Write on the label in ballpoint pen once the label is on the disk;
- Use pencil to write labels – the graphite might corrupt the disk;
- Leave disks lying around where they could be mishandled or have things spilt on them.

Some equipment can be affected by fluctuations in the power supply; special surge protectors can be obtained to combat this.

Some equipment needs a 'clean' power line into which other electrical appliances (e.g. vacuum cleaners) must not be plugged. Check with the equipment supplier.

Cleaning kits for screens and disk drive heads are available and are advertised in computer accessory magazines. Screen cleaning kits can also be used for photocopier glass plates

Cables, junctions etc. should be carefully routed and encased in trunking where necessary *(See 4.6)*.

Static can be minimised by anti-static solution on carpets, anti-static mats etc.; these are advertised in computer accessory magazines.

If your equipment does go wrong, make a note of all that happened and everything you did. It will help the engineer diagnose and repair the fault. Keep a careful note of intermittent faults, which are the most difficult to diagnose. A Computer Fault Book, logging all faults and action taken, is a good idea – the same applies to photocopiers *(See 1.6)*.

3.3 Computer terminology

The following glossary of terms is made up of computer terminology normally used in the office, as opposed to a computer department. It has a bias towards word processing terms.

Abbreviation file The facility to give abbreviations to often-repeated words and phrases, so that when the abbreviation is keyed in, the whole word or phrase will appear.

ABORT Means stop.

Acoustic hood A 'hood', usually made of plastic, which goes over the printer to cut down the noise.

Alpha/numeric sort The facility to sort lists, etc., alphabetically or numerically, ascending or descending.

Amend To make corrections and alterations to a text already keyed in.

Anti-static A spray, mat or other medium which will reduce the static electricity in the atmosphere.

ASCII The American Standard Code for Information Interchange. It is a well-known machine code.

Automatic page numbering A facility which allows you to give commands to number pages automatically, according to your needs.

Background Processes go on 'in the background' while you are using the screen for something else. For example, one document can be 'background' printed while you are keying in another document.

Back-up Systematic copying and secure storage of information on copy disks. The second copy is often called a *Security Disk*.

BASIC A computer language. Stands for Beginners All-purpose Symbolic Instruction Code.

Binary The code in which computers work, consisting of combinations of 0's and 1's.

Bit Each coded 0 or 1 in the binary system.

Block move The function of moving a block of text from one part of a document to another. Also known as *cut and paste*.

Boiler-plating Merging pre-stored documents or paragraphs together to make one required document.

Boot To 'boot' is to set the system going – pull it up by its boot straps.

Buffer Temporary memory where data is stored before processing.

Bug A program error.

Byte Short for 'by eight'. 8 bits = 1 byte.

Carbon ribbons High quality ribbons which can be used only once.

Cartridge disks 'Hard' disks encased in plastic with a large memory capacity.

Centring   The ability to centre text between the margins.

Character   Any letter, figures, symbol or space which can be displayed.

COBOL   COmmon Business Orientated Language – a computer language.

Column manipulation   The facility to move tabulated columns around the screen.

3.3 Computer terminology

Command driven   The software is controlled by special command words keyed in by the user.

Commands   Messages keyed in to command the computer to execute the required function.

Command strings   Strings of words, phrases, etc. that can be called to the screen by giving the correct commands.

Configuration   The whole hardware set-up of the system – terminals, CPUs and peripherals.

Continuous stationery   Stationery which can be fed through the printer continuously, like traditional computer paper.

CPU   Central Processing Unit – the central control unit of any computer.

CRT   Cathode Ray Tube. Sometimes used to mean the screen.

Cursor   The (often) flashing square, oblong or line which tells you where you are on the screen.

Cut and leave   The function of putting text into temporary memory and using it in another part of the document, while leaving the original where it is.

Cut and paste   The function of moving text from one part of the document and 'pasting' it in to another. Also known as *block move*.

Daisy wheel   The print head made of plastic or metal which looks like a daisy, with a character on each petal.

Daisy wheel printers   Printers which use daisy wheels and which produce high-quality printout.

Data   Any information, figures and words which are to be processed into meaningful material.

Dedicated WP   A system 'dedicated' almost entirely to word (not data) processing.

Default   The values (for margins, pitch, etc.) pre-set in the software. The system will 'default to' the pre-set value unless instructed otherwise.

Device   The various parts of the configuration. Can be a printer or a disk drive or a screen. 'Device not ready' probably means something is not switched on.

Diagnostic   Used to find faults – often refers to disks which an engineer uses.

Disk   The storage media used by many computers – hard, floppy and Winchester are examples.

Disk drive   The part of the computer which 'reads' the information on the disks. This is where the disks are inserted.

Document assembly   The process of creating names or numbered paragraphs which can be stored and then called to the screen by keying in the appropriate name or number.

Dot matrix printer   The printer has a battery of pins which create characters from a pattern of dots.

Double columns   Two columns of work, each of which is an entity and can be amended, justified, etc., without affecting work in the other column.

Electronic mail   A service which allows computer terminals to dial up over the telephone network to consult personal electronic mailboxes. Used for sending messages between computers.

Embolden   To embolden is to command the printer to overprint two to four times so that the print appears in bold type.

Enhance   To enhance a system is to buy further, normally more powerful, devices or software to add on to the existing system.

EXIT   A command often used to get out of a program.

Fabric ribbons   Ribbons made of nylon fabric for use in daisy wheel printers. Can be used until too faint.

Field   A specific area on the screen or in a document – on a form you have a 'field' for the name, address, etc.

File   A named 'document' created and held in the computer's memory.

Floppy disk   A round disk in a square protective casing which is flexible – hence floppy. Comes in various sizes ($3\frac{1}{2}''$, $5\frac{1}{4}''$, $8''$).

Floppy disk drive   A drive in which you insert floppy disks.

Footers   Page numbers and other information, such as footnotes, found at the bottom of a page.

Font   The typeface or printstyle. Each printer can use several different fonts, depending on the power of the software.

Format   To format – to prepare or initialize a disk. A format – the way a document is set up (margins, tabs, etc.).

FORTRAN   A computer language particularly used by mathematicians (from FORmula TRANslator).

Function keys Keys additional to the normal alpha-numerical keys on the keyboard which allow you to perform specific WP functions.

GIGO A commonly used equation:
Garbage In = Garbage Out – in other words if you input rubbish, then rubbish will be produced and printed out.

Global search and replace The facility to search out, automatically, throughout a document, a word or phrase and replace it with another.

GO A command often used to set a system going.

Hard copy Printout (on paper).

Hard disk A large round disk encased in plastic. Also called a *cartridge disk*. Has large memory capacity.

Hardware The mechanical, electronic and plastic pieces of a computer. If you can touch it, it's hardware.

Headers Headings, page numbers and other information found at the top of each page.

HELP A facility on many systems which helps you to diagnose where you have gone wrong and put matters right.

Highlight To 'highlight' a word, sentence, etc. on the screen means to define/delineate the word, sentence, etc. with which you wish to deal.

Hot zone The region at the end of each line so many characters in from the right-hand margin. The zone can be set by the operator. Words within this zone require hyphenation, or will be wrapped round.

Index The catalogue or list of documents/files stored on a disk.

Initialize To 'prepare' a blank disk for use on a specific system.

Input/output (I/O) Input is the information fed into the computer. Output is the information produced by the computer.

Interface A specially-constructed box and/or cable which allows different parts of the computer to communicate with each other.

Justification The right-hand margin, like the left, is 'justified' so that it is printed out with a straight right-hand margin. The characters are spaced out to fill up the line, as in true printing.

K Literally, a thousand. There are 1024 bytes in a Kilobyte (K).

Used to express the amount of memory available on a system – for example 32K, 64K, etc.

Language Writing programs in binary, which the computer understands, is too difficult and cumbersome. Therefore languages (e.g. BASIC, COBOL, FORTRAN), which are more like English, allow programmers to write more easily. Programs are written in these languages and then translated (by the computer) into binary or 'machine' code.

Laser printer Printer which uses laser beams; very quiet and versatile; produces top quality printouts.

List processing The facility to merge, for example, names and addresses with a 'form' or standard letter and print out. Often called *mail merge*.

LOGON/LOGOFF A phrase often used on mainframe computers, and WP packages attached to them, asking you to 'log on' – in other words enter the program. Similarly used to exit from the program.

Mail merge The facility to merge, for example, names and addresses with a 'form' or standard letter. The letter only has to be keyed in once. The merge and printing takes place automatically. Sometimes called *list processing*.

Mainframe A powerful computer of large capacity and versatility, usually used by large organisations.

Maths pack A program which allows the operator to do simple mathematical calculations on the computer.

Memory A measure of the power of the computer is its memory capacity. 132K means that the computer has the capacity for 132 thousand bytes of memory.

Menu Alternatives presented to the user on the screen so that the required function can be selected. Menu-based systems are normally easier to use than command-based systems.

Micro The smallest of the computers. Can usually do word and data processing, but not simultaneously.

Mini A smaller version of a mainframe computer. Can usually do word and data processing simultaneously.

Modem Short for modulator/demodulator. It enables you to attach your computer to a telephone line, translating computer signals into those used by the telephone network.

Moderate Means to alter (text). You can re-call a document to the screen, moderate it, and file it away again in the computer's memory – or print it out.

Mouse A free-moving device which moves the cursor on the screen to required positions.
Move The facility to move text around the screen.
Multi-strike High-quality carbon ribbons.

NLQ Near Letter Quality: a function on a dot matrix printer allowing near letter quality printouts.
Numeric pad The layout of numeric keys usually on a pad to the right of the main keyboard. Sometimes incorporated in the main keyboard.

Operating system The 'heart' of the software. It ensures the correct interpretation of commands, etc.
Operator disk The disk on which the main word processing (or other) software program is stored to make the system work. Often called the *system disk*.
Optical character reader (OCR) A machine which can 'read' typescript directly into a word processor. Can usually only read specified fonts.

Pagination The facility to break a long document into given page lengths (usually between 55 and 60 lines to an A4 page).
Peripherals The printers, disk drives, keyboards, etc. which enable information and programs to be fed in and out of a computer.
Print setting The margins (top, bottom, left and right) and page length set for a page of printout.
Printwheel Another name for a daisy wheel.
Program The instructions written to make the machine obey certain commands, etc. Note the spelling.

QWERTY The name given to the familiar typewriter keyboard – from the first six letters on the top line of alpha keys.

RAM Random Access Memory.
Read/write commands Commands given to the word processor to 'read' a document or 'write' it to disk.
ROM Read Only Memory.

SAVE To 'file' the work created on the screen on disk, or other storage medium, or in a temporary memory.
Scratch file A facility for putting text into temporary memory.

Scrolling The action of moving the text up and down the screen, and to left and right.

Search and replace The facility to find a word or phrase throughout a document so that the operator can replace it with another word or phrase. Often called *selective search and replace* (see also *global search and replace*).

Security disk A second back-up copy of a disk.

Shared logic A hardware system where several terminals share the CPU, software and printers.

Single sheet feeder A device attached to the printer which will automatically feed in single sheets of paper.

Software Refers to all programs run on computer hardware – the instructions which make the machine work.

Split screen The facility to call up parts of two pages on the screen at the same time. The screen is split to allow for this.

Standalone A small hardware system which is complete in itself, comprising VDU, CPU, disk drives, keyboard and printer.

Status line The line, usually at the extreme top or bottom of a screen, which shows the 'status' of the work – line number, character number, etc.

Storage disk The disk on which is stored the work you have created. Sometimes called a *work disk*.

SYNTAX ERROR A phrase used to tell you that you have keyed in something incorrectly.

System disk The disk on which the main word processing (or other) program is stored to make the 'system' work. You cannot boot the system up without it. Sometimes called a *software* or an *operator disk*.

Terminal The screen and keyboard together make a terminal.

Thimble A type of print 'wheel' shaped like a thimble.

Tractor feeder An accessory which clips on top of the printer to ensure that continuous stationery goes in straight.

Turnkey A system installed for you, normally by a consultant, which is 'up and running' and ready to go. You only have to 'turn the key'.

Unbundle Systems are often sold as a total package – hardware, software, training, etc. To 'unbundle' is to sell each part separately.

User friendly This means that the system should be easy to use and that the messages on the screen are clear and comprehensible, and not written in computer jargon.

VDU Visual Display Unit – the screen.

Wide screen A facility which allows you to extend the right-hand margin beyond the normal 80. The screen itself remains the same size.

3.3 Computer terminology
3.4 Electronic diaries
3.5 Electronic mail

Widows and orphans These occur when printing out long documents. The page number, etc., appears at the top of the next page (the orphan) instead of the bottom of the correct page (the widow).

Winchester Disk A small compact hard disk unit often found with micros.

Work disk The disk (of whatever type) on which you store the work you have created. Also called a *storage disk*.

Workstation The place where an operator sits and works – includes desk, chair, terminal, etc.

Wraparound The facility which automatically transfers a word that is too long for the line onto the next line. No need to use the RETURN key.

3.4 Electronic diaries

If you are on a *network (See 3.7)* it is possible to keep diaries electronically. You can:

- Create as many diaries as you please to record details of appointments etc. You could create a special diary for meeting room bookings, allowing all users on the network to access that diary.
- Look at other people's diaries to check free times, provided you have the users' permission.
- Co-ordinate several diaries to book a meeting for several people.

As with any other diary, this system is useless if diaries are not up-to-date.

3.5 Electronic mail

3.5.1 Electronic mail services
Electronic mail services work rather like the Post Office – except that messages are stored electronically in a central computer. When

you dial up the service you are told if there are any messages waiting for you, and you can choose to read them at once or wait for a while.

This means that you can send messages to anyone whose mailbox 'address' you know; you can send them at whatever time of day you want, knowing that they will be in the recipient's mailbox within minutes. You can send them without having to speak to the recipient in person – although you can ask to be notified automatically (via your own mailbox) when your message has been received.

The major drawback is that the people you want to talk to must also be electronic mail users. What is more, there are four principal British electronic mail suppliers and as yet there is no communication between them. So not only must the people you want to mail be electronic mail users, they must also be on the same system.

PROS:
  – Within minutes
  – No stamps or postboxes
  – Can be acknowledged
  – One 'mailing' can reach several people at once
  – 24 hour service
  – Might be cheaper than first-class mail
  – Has telex option *(See 3.5.2)*

CONS:
  – Correspondent must be a mailbox user
  – Must be on the same system
  – Extra initial cost
  – More expensive than second-class mail

3.5.2　*Electronic mail Telex*
(For Telex see 3.19)

A major plus is that some of the electronic mail services can also be used (at an extra charge) to send and receive Telexes.

You save the cost of the Telex terminal, and you also save most of the other Telex charges. For an occasional user, an electronic mail service with the Telex option can be highly cost-effective.

For information, contact electronic equipment suppliers, particularly those concerned with networks *(See 3.7)*.

3.6　FAX

FAX is short for facsimile; facsimile copies of documents can be transmitted almost anywhere in the world. The document is fed into the transmitting machine where it is 'read' by the machine and converted into 'language' which is understood by telephone apparatus. It is then sent via the telephone lines to the receiving FAX machine and 'translated' back into the image that a human being can understand.

| 3.5 Electronic mail |
| 3.6 FAX |
| 3.7 Networks and cables |

Copies of documents, illustrations, diagrams, sketches, photographs etc can be transmitted in this manner. Compatible machines are required at both ends of the communication channel, linked by a telephone line. FAX users normally print their FAX number on their company stationery.

Features to look out for:

- Automatic dialling: frequently-used numbers can be fed in so that the press of one button can call the number and start transmission.
- Automatic re-dialling if the number is busy or does not answer; after a given number of times automatic printout reporting on what has happened.
- Auto-timer: deferred transmission/polling allows you to send or request automatically at any time during the day or night, without an operator.
- Quality of printout.
- Transmission and reduction of oversize documents.
- No telephone receiver required.
- If telephone is connected, transmitter can send a signal to receiver to pick up the phone when the transaction is completed so that verbal confirmation can be given.
- Automatic document feeder.
- On a network, a multiple polling capability, collecting all required documents automatically, say overnight.
- Full printout of FAX transactions.

3.7   Networks and cables

3.7.1   Networks

Networks, local networks and local area networks are all the same thing. Information is transmitted back and forth to a multiplicity of work stations by cable. What can be connected to what? It could be:

- one computer to another;
- several terminals connected to one printer, or one large storage disk;
- individual terminals connected through an access point to an external service like Prestel *(See 3.11)* or a database run by a local authority, for example.

Networks can share devices as well as information, such as printers, access to a modem *(See Computer terminology 3.3)*, or large-capacity disks.

Imagine being able to call up any information in your building on your terminal, process it, store it, print it out, transmit it or do anything else you need to do with it, and it becomes apparent that a network is the key to real office automation.

3.7.2 Cables
Networks depend on cables. Cables must:

- be the right sort of cable to make the connection
- have the right sort of plugs at both ends
- be in the right position
- be properly connected
- not be a safety hazard *(See 4.6)*

There are very many different sorts of cables and plugs; for different types of cable and connectors see any computer accessory magazine and consult your equipment supplier.

3.8   Optical Character Readers (OCRs)

An OCR machine 'reads' pages of typescript directly into a computer, particularly a word processor, so you can use this machine to input text instead of keying it in through the keyboard.

Some OCR machines can read any print style or font, but many can read only specific fonts. Look out for:

- A variey of readable fonts
- Acceptable formats (e.g. margins, justified text, number of lines per page etc.)
- Reading speed
- Reading accuracy
- Paper sizes it will accommodate
- Colours it cannot read
- Methods of paper feed
- Ease of control panel

3.9 Paging machines

Paging machines are useful for keeping in touch with people who are often 'mobile' during the course of their work.

Basically there are two types of machine:

(*a*)   The machine which can contact you through a bleeper; when it bleeps you know you have to make contact via the nearest telephone. These machines are very useful within a building.

(*b*)   The radiopager which can contact you at very great distances. The pager will bleep and a short message appears on your small display screen, e.g. 'Ring the office' or 'Go to Heathrow'.

Radiopagers and other paging systems are sold by British Telecom and other communications suppliers.

3.10 Photocopiers

(For Photocopying Tips see 1.6)

3.10.1 Photocopier features

Features now available with many photocopiers include the following.

Automatic sheet feed   Originals (perhaps a document several pages long) can be fed in automatically, page by page.

Double-sided copying   The paper is automatically turned over while your originals are being automatically fed in.

Collating multiple copies   An attachment at the output end will collate your copies in the right order into sets. Even quite a small copier can have a 15-bin collator as an attachment.

Differing paper sizes   Most copiers can cope with A5, A4 and A3 paper *(for Paper sizes See 9.4)*.

Reduction and enlargement   Quite compact desk-top models can reduce and enlarge the size of your typescript or picture.

Processing parts of a page   Some sophisticated copiers can move selected parts of a page (the relevant part of a map, for example) to a different position on another sheet of paper, and enlarge or reduce it as necessary. They can also squeeze and stretch things into different shapes.

Memory   Given the right commands, the copier can store instructions, say for reduction or enlargement, in its memory and reproduce exactly what you want at any time.

Two-page separation   Lay one A3 page or two A4 pages side by side on the glass plate and the copier will copy each page separately; magazines or books can be copied if they are equivalent to one A3 page, but watch the copyright laws.

Links with word processors and other computers   Computers can be linked direct to the photocopier, so your printouts can be automatically produced several times over from the same terminal.

Colour   Colour (a limited range as yet) has been in photocopying for a little time now. It does require you to change the toner containers to get the different colours.

Copying onto acetate sheets   Useful for making slides for the overhead projector from paper originals, either text or diagrams. It is often easier to draw the originals on paper and then transfer to acetate, rather than work directly onto acetate sheets. A general drawback is loss of colour; to produce several colours would mean passing the acetate sheet through the copier several times.

3.10.2   Photocopier control

Three main methods of controlling the use of the photocopier are:

- A book for recording transactions;
- A 'credit card' which allows you to activate the machine and make copies up to the number allowed on your card;
- A computer program which records every transaction electronically, allocates costs for departmental and personal use and prints out reports for management and to support invoices.

3.11   Prestel

Prestel is a national database – British Telecom's Videotex service – which is accessed through the telephone and a special Prestel adaptor on a computer terminal. It cannot be accessed through your television set.

Prestel can be used for such things as home and office banking, home shopping, booking holidays, booking theatre tickets, travel bookings etc, i.e. it is interactive, unlike teletext *(See 3.18)* which is purely an information service. Prestel also has hundreds of thousands of pages of information.

Charges are made for the use of this service according to the service required and the time used.

For further information on Prestel call the Prestel Enquiry Bureau on 01-822 1122.

3.10 Photocopiers
3.11 Prestel
3.12 Radiophones

3.12 Radiophones

In-car cellular telephones have two rival systems – Cellnet (BT/Securicor) and Vodafone (Racal) – both linked in to BT's telephone network system.

These two suppliers are not allowed to supply the telephones themselves, so any mobile telephone you buy will link up to either system.

There are three basic types:

– The 'mobile' unit, fixed into the car.
– The 'hand-portable' which runs on batteries and can be used in or out of the car; not recommended for use while actually driving.
– The 'transportable' which can plug into the car's power supply and be moved from car to car.

Look for these features:

– Push button dialling, last-number recall, an electronic lock to prevent unauthorised use of the phone;
– Large number memories;
– Facility to input a number into the memory during a call;
– 'Call-referral' – incoming calls can be automatically directed to another number;
– 'Conference call' which allows more than two phones to be connected up at the same time;
– Ability to link a personal computer to a company mainframe;
– 'Hands-off' facility, which allows the driver to leave the phone in its cradle and speak through a mike – much the safest for calling while driving.

Check initial costs, peak, standard and cheap times – they vary – and costs per minute.

3.13   Switchboards

Switchboards are now more commonly called PBXs (Private Branch Exchange) or PABx (Private Automatic Branch Exchange). They provide the points at which an internal phone system connects to British Telecom's services. *(See also Radiophones 3.12, telephone techniques 1.9 and telephones 3.16.)*
Features can include:

- automatic retries if the number you are calling is engaged;
- automatic re-routeing: calls can be diverted to an alternative number;
- verification: allowing only authorised users to make long-distance calls, for example;
- teleconferencing and party calls – several people in different locations participate in a 'meeting' by phone;
- 'voicegrams': voice messages are recorded and stored until the recipient gets back to listen to them;
- dictation storage: dictation is given over the phone and stored until allocated to a typist;
- call logging and telephone management: finding out which extensions are making what kind of calls, when and how long the calls last;
- automatic queuing of incoming calls;
- music while on 'hold';
- large number memory.

The PBX can also provide the central control for other facilities that use the telephone lines, e.g. data communications or FAX. Instead of connecting your computer or FAX machine directly to a phone line, it could be plugged in to the internal phone system. The PBX would then handle the allocation of a phone line and dial the number automatically; it could also monitor the call and provide a costed summary of usage.

3.14   Teleconferences

(See also 6.1.3)

These can be by phone *(See 3.13)*, in-car phone *(See Radiophones 3.12)*, or by closed-circuit television links.
Meetings can follow formal meeting formats *(See Unit 6)* or be informal 'ad hoc' meetings.
For formal meetings preparations are much the same as for

normal formal meetings, except that
the communications link has to be
established at a certain time – and
needs to be booked beforehand.

Charges are fairly high, so that the
meeting needs to be efficiently and
effectively conducted. The Chair must
remember that via television partici-
pants can see each other, but via telephone they cannot. One party
may not know that another has left the room. Consideration needs
to be given to keeping all participants informed of what is going on
(See also 1.9.6), and keeping the conversation flowing in an in-
formative way.

3.15 Telemessages

These are messages which can be passed or held electronically
instead of by hard copy (paper).

Messages can be left via the Electronic Mail service *(See 3.5)*, or
via a network *(See 3.7)* or as a Voicegram *(See 3.13)* or on an
Answering Machine *(See 3.1)*.

If on a network, beware response time (the time it takes to get the
screen to call up your message). If someone, for example, is using a
WP program and wants to access a message, the response time can
be slow. People have found it better to leave one terminal in
'message' mode and use that terminal for other programs only when
necessary.

A Telemessage is also the word used for telegrams sent by phone
(See BT Services 3.16).

3.16 Telephones and British Telecom services

3.16.1 Telephones
(See also Switchboards 3.13)

Telephones are not a BT monopoly and can be bought from
equipment suppliers and many retail outlets. Look for the green
circle, which denotes an instrument approved for connection
to BT's networks. Instruments marked with a red triangle are
prohibited from direct or indirect connection to public telecommunications systems.

Telephones which operate via a PBX *(See 3.13)* can use all the facilities available on the switchboard. In addition, features available on small and private telephone systems include:

- Dialling memory
- Last-number re-dial
- Hands-free dialling via mike and loudspeaker
- Ringing volume adjustment
- Push-button dialling

QWERTYphones incorporate a QWERTY keyboard and an LCD (liquid crystal display). Features include:

- A memotyper: a single-line editor which allows the preparation of memos. Each completed line can be stored for later transmission, either to a local printer or to another QWERTYphone.
- A call timer.
- Access to database and mailbox systems.
- Directory facilities with autodialling and directory search capability.

This is a product of British Telecom Business Systems.

3.16.2   British Telecom services
British Telecom services for business and private use are advertised in The Phone Book and include:

- Operator Services: dial 100
- Directory Enquiries: dial 142 from London to London
                                                192 for all other numbers
- Emergency Calls: dial 999
- Fault Repair Service: dial 151
- Telemessages *(See 3.15)*: dial 190 from London
                                                100 from elsewhere
- International Telemessages: dial 193 from London
                                                100 from elsewhere
- International Telegrams: dial 193 from London
                                                100 from elsewhere
- Maritime Services: dial 100
- Any other call enquiries: dial 191

Dial 150 for enquiries and information on:

- Business Systems, such as:
     Voicebank (receives and sends messages)
     Stofor (store and forward message systems)

IPSS (International Packet
Switching Service)
Freefone (Customer contacts
company through operator)
0800 Service (Customer contacts
company direct)
- Consumer Product Sales
- Your Phone Bill – ask for Telephone
  Accounts
- Customer Service – for unresolved problems
- Phone Books/Directories – Phone Book Entries or Phone Book
  Supplies
- Call Charges – free leaflet explaining charges
- Radiophones *(See 3.12)*
- Prestel *(See 3.11)*
- Radiopaging *(See 3.9)*
- FAX *(See 3.6)*

3.16 Telephone services
3.17 Teletex

3.16.3 *British Telecom information services*

Consult your local Phone Book for numbers for the following and
other 'entertainment' services.

British Gas Recipeline	Recipes
Cricket line	Test match scores, etc.
Eventline	Motor sport information
FT Cityline	Financial information
Newsline	News bulletin updated hourly
Leisureline	Selection of main events
Marineline	Marine information
Skiline	Scottish ski information
Sportsline	General sports roundup
Timeline	The speaking clock
Traveline	Road, Rail, Air and Sea services
Weatherline	Weather information
William Hill Raceline	Horse racing results and information

3.17   Teletex (no final 't')

A kind of super Telex *(See 3.19)*, done by computer. It uses
different connections, works faster and allows capital letters and
lower-case letters to be used.

Teletex terminals are expensive and not yet widely used.

3.18   Teletext (with final 't')

This is the information service available through your television –
nothing to do with Telex or Teletex.

Ceefax is the BBC service and Oracle the ITA service.

Useful for travel information *(See Unit 11)*, stock exchange prices
etc.

It can only be accessed through a television set which has the
teletext feature.

It is not interactive – you cannot make travel bookings, book
theatre seats etc. This can be done via Prestel *(See 3.11)*.

3.19   Telex

Telex is a way of sending information in text form – rather like the
telephone system in that you can contact another person almost
anywhere in the world, provided they have the right equipment.
You use text rather than your voice. Telex users usually have their
Telex number on their company stationery.

Telex is comparatively slow, and you can only use capital letters,
although modern Telex machines are a great improvement. Look
for the following features:

- Facility for making repeated attempts to contact a given num-
  ber, anywhere in the world;
- Multi-address: for sending the same message to different
  addresses;
- Pre-recorded Address (PRA) list facility;
- Personalised messages – the Telex gets to the right person.

The public Telex service is run by British Telecom. Computers
can also be used as Telex machines, provided they are BT approved.
Information from network *(See 3.7)* suppliers.

3.20   Word processing

For a detailed study of word processing, see *Teach Yourself Word
Processing*. This book does not deal with specific machines, but with
the principles of word processing, hardware, software, disk management etc. (For word processing terminology, see *Computer
terminology 3.3.)*

If you are thinking of installing word processing, try following this
sequence:

(a) Must your WP be *compatible* with another machine? If so, start by finding out about the compatible software and hardware.

3.18 Telextext
3.19 Telex
3.20 Word processing

(b) Think about the type of *work* you will want to do on a WP. This will determine what sort of software package you have.

(c) Make a list of what is *essential* in your *software* package (e.g. double-column work) and what is *desirable* (e.g. alphabetic sort). Buy only a software package which contains all the essentials.

(d) Think about the type of *printer* required – dot matrix, daisy wheel, ink jet or laser – the quality of the output depends on the type of printer.

(e) Think about the *hardware*: ease of keyboard, disk drive, screen colour, portability etc.

(f) Think about *storage disks*: floppy, mini floppy, Winchester, cartridge.

(g) Think about the *accessories*: e.g. daisy wheels, ribbons, continuous stationery, labels, disk storage containers etc.

(h) Read the *documentation* that goes with the machine and see if you can begin to understand it. Is training included in your purchase?

(i) Think about *maintenance agreements*.

The legal aspects of health and safety at work are dealt with under Section **5.5**.

4.1   Accident Book

4.1.1   Notifiable accidents
All industrial accidents, including those which occur in offices, must be recorded in an Accident Book. This is a *legal requirement (See 5.5)*.

An accident is notifiable if:

- Death is caused;
- Serious personal injury is caused;
- The victim is off work for 3 or more successive days;
- There is a 'near miss' – a dangerous occurrence has taken place.

4.1.2   Regulations
For details of regulations see *Notification of Accidents and Dangerous Occurrences Regulations 1980* SI 804.

A guidance note on these regulations can be obtained from the Health & Safety Executive: *Booklet HS(R)S*.

A form for making an Accident Report is obtainable from the Health & Safety Executive. (*For address see 12.12*)

4.1.3   Accident Reports and entries in the Accident Book
An *Accident Report* must show:

- Date
- Full details of person making report
- Circumstances of accident
- Details of employer's relevant safety policy
- Estimated cause of accident (by someone qualified to judge)
- Recommendations to avoid repeat
- Signature

An entry in the *Accident Book* must show

- Name, sex, age, occupation of victim
- Nature of injury and place where it occurred
- Description of circumstances

The record must be kept at the place of work for 3 years.

Accidents must be recorded as soon as possible after the accident happens, before memory fails and facts get distorted. This is partly to substantiate any future compensation claims, and partly to establish any pattern of accidents which emerges.

4.2 Fire precautions

Make sure all electrical appliances are properly wired and insulated.

Do not smoke in non-smoking areas.

Use metal (not wicker) waste paper baskets.

Keep fire exits clear.

Keep fire doors shut.

Check fire extinguishers regularly.

Have training in the use of the correct fire extinguishers.

Have regular fire drills.

Make sure everyone knows what to do in case of fire.

Do not use electric bar fires, however cold it is.

Do not cover electric convector heaters.

Have fire exits clearly signed.

Test fire bells regularly.

Follow procedures for noting who is in the building – visitors' books *(See 1.8)*, staff attendance lists etc.

4.3 First Aid

It is a legal requirement that companies with 150 or more employees must have a qualified first aider available. St John Ambulance Brigade run one-week courses for people to obtain this qualification.

Generally only trained first aiders should deal with serious accidents, but personal first aid knowledge can often minimise the effects of an accident and sometimes even save a life.

For a full and clear description of what to do see the *First Aid Manual*, published jointly by The British Red Cross Society, St John Ambulance Brigade and St Andrew's Ambulance Association. (See the Phone Book for local numbers. The book is obtainable from book shops.) In particular study the sections on the recovery position and dealing with shock.

Some basic dos and don'ts for accidents most likely to occur in the office:

Minor Cuts
- Wash your hands before dealing with a cut
- Rinse the wound clean under lightly running water
- Cover with adhesive dressing

Bruises and sprains
- Place injured area under cold running water
- If injury is in an awkward place raise and support the injured part
- Apply a cold compress – towel or cloth soaked in cold water and wrung out so it is damp but not dripping

Electrical injuries
- Break the electrical current by switching off at mains if possible
- If not possible, stand on something dry and insulating (wood, rubber, newspaper) and push victim away from power source with brush, wooden chair etc.
- *Do not* use anything metal or damp
- *Do not* touch the victim's flesh until you know the electrical contact has been broken
- Call an ambulance
- Attend to electrical burn if possible

Electrical burns
- Put a pad of clean, non-fluffy material over the burn and secure it with a bandage
- *Do not* apply lotions, ointments or fat
- *Do not* break blisters, remove loose skin or touch injured area
- Call an ambulance

Scalds
- Place injured part under slowly-running cold water (use any cold liquid – e.g. milk, beer – if water is not available)
- Remove rings, watches and other constrictions from area before it starts to swell
- Put on a pad of clean, non-fluffy material and secure with a bandage
- *Do not* use adhesive dressings
- *Do not* break blisters, remove loose skin or touch injured area
- *Do not* apply lotions, ointments or fat

*Heart attack (Chest *pains, ashen skin, giddiness, sweating, breathlessness)*
If you suspect someone is having a heart attack

- Put person in half-sitting position (not lying down) with head and shoulders supported and knees bent
- *Do not* allow the person to move unnecessarily
- Loosen constricting clothing
- Call an ambulance

*Stroke (*Head *pains, confusion, giddiness)*
- Lie person down on back with head and shoulders slightly raised and supported. Position head on side to allow saliva to drain from mouth.
- Loosen constricting clothing
- Call an ambulance

Note: for a full description of heart attack and stroke symptoms, see the *First Aid Manual.*

4.4   First Aid Box

The First Aid Box should always be available and topped up with its full complement of supplies. One designated person (with a deputy) should be in charge of it.

The First Aid Box as recommended in the *First Aid Manual* should contain:

- 10 individually wrapped adhesive dressings (plasters)
- 1 sterile eye pad with attachment
- 1 triangular bandage
- 1 sterile covering for a serious wound
- 6 safety pins
- 3 medium sized sterile unmedicated dressings
- 1 large sterile unmedicated dressing
- 1 extra large sterile unmedicated dressing
- 1 pair of scissors
- 1 pair of tweezers

Antiseptic cream should be used for minor cuts only.

4.3 First Aid
4.4 First Aid Box

4.5   Harassment: where to go for help

4.5.1   *What is it?*

The term 'harassment' covers a wide range of behaviour. Towards the lesser end of the scale it includes unwelcome sexual comments or jokes; in its more serious forms it can include sexual assault and rape. The common factor is that the woman objects to the man's words and/or actions which are directed at her and are either blatantly or implicitly sexual. Both women and men can be victims of harassment but, as women are more often on the receiving end, the following section will refer to women.

4.5.2   *What can be done about it?*

Harassment in an office, both sexual and mental, can be really distressing and cause lack of efficiency at work. It can also strain working relationships to breaking point. The important thing is not to keep quiet about it, but to seek help and advice if you cannot deal with the problem yourself.

In a large organisation your Personnel Department should be able to help. You may, however, have to approach this department through your Manager, who may be the cause of the problem in the first place.

The law can also be of help. It is possible to take an employer to an Industrial Tribunal to get a declaration that the behaviour is unlawful and possibly to obtain compensation.

There are two legal routes. If the harassment is so bad that the victim feels she cannot do the same job any more and resigns she could then claim constructive unfair dismissal. This is effectively claiming that the employee has been forced to leave the job. *(See 5.3.1)* (See also 'Sex Discrimination Decisions No. 16' from the Equal Opportunities Commission.)

Alternatively, the woman could pursue a claim under the Sex Discrimination Act 1975. This Act says it is unlawful to treat a woman worse than a man would be treated in the same or similar situation. This evidently covers such treatment as sexual harassment. So, if the woman can show that a man would not be subjected to such treatment this amounts to showing that there has been unlawful discrimination. If the harassment has had tangible consequences such as transfer, disciplinary proceedings against the woman, loss of promotion or training opportunities, then it is easier to prove that the woman has suffered. However, it can still be difficult to prove the connection between the harassment and these sorts of consequences.

'Rights Of Women' produce a leaflet giving advice on ways of coping with harassment *(for address see 12.12)*.

The TUC has published a leaflet called 'Sexual Harassment at Work' *(for address see 12.12)*.

Other groups to contact for help include the Equal Opportunities Commission and Women Against Sexual Harassment *(for addresses see 12.12)*.

In some areas there is a local *Helpline* which you can phone, in or out of office hours. For your local service look in the blue Community pages of your Thomson's Directory *(See 12.7)* to find the most appropriate *Helpline* for you. Failing that, try the library, the Citizens Advice Bureau or the Samaritans, who will tell you where to find the specific help you need.

4.6 Hazards in the office

As well as the fire precautions to be taken *(See 4.2)*, avoid the main causes of accidents in the office by following the tips given below.

Trailing cables and wires cause tripping; make sure all cables and wires are secured, are in trunking where necessary *(See 3.2)* and do not run where people can trip over them.

Open cupboard doors and cabinet drawers are obstructions; close them when not in use.

Never open an upper drawer of a filing cabinet when a lower one is open; the cabinet could topple over.

Do not leave piles of paper and files in walkways; people could fall over them.

Have sensible arrangements for making hot drinks; do not put cups and mugs of hot liquids where they can be knocked over.

Do not let jewellery and ties or scarves dangle in moving parts of equipment, e.g. printers.

Keep your fingers out of moving parts of equipment; turn off electrical appliances at the mains before trying to mend or unjam them.

Observe the precautions for unjamming paper in the photocopier. Some parts of the machine get very hot.

Do not carry things which are too heavy for you; get help or use a lifting and moving device (e.g. a trolley for moving a typewriter).

When lifting heavy items from the floor (boxes of paper, perhaps) bend your knees, feet firmly on the ground, spine straight, chin in; take the strain on your legs, not your back.

Do not stand on chairs, particularly swivel chairs, to reach things which are high up. Use a stool or steps.

If using sprays, like spraymount, or other chemicals, make sure there is adequate ventilation.

Smoking can permanently damage your health; in an enclosed environment, it can also damage the health of others (passive smoking).

4.7   VDUs

People fear that prolonged use of VDUs will cause many aches, pains and even permanent damage. There are various *Health and Safety Executive* publications on this issue, giving the latest research findings, advice and guidance. *(For address see 12.12.)*

4.7.1   Pregnancy
There is a fear of birth abnormalities, but there is no firm evidence that VDUs are a health hazard to pregnant women. Radiation from VDUs (the equivalent to that from a hair dryer or an electric blanket) does *not* appear to be a cause of birth abnormalities.

Stress through fear of working with VDUs can cause problems, as can badly-designed work stations. If you are pregnant and worried about working with VDUs, let your manager know. Any reasonable employer will treat the matter sympathetically.

4.7.2   Eyestrain
People do complain of eyestrain and headaches after prolonged use of VDUs, but there is no evidence that VDU use damages the eyes. It is much more likely that spectacles are not worn when they are needed, or that incorrect spectacles are worn (bi-focals can be a particular problem), or that workstation design and job content is at fault. If in any doubt at all:

– have your eyes tested by an optician who knows about VDUs;
– check the workstation design, particularly for glare *(See 4.7.3)*;
– consider the job rotation and whether you are spending too long

at the VDU without a break. VDU work is very concentrated, which in itself can cause stress and fatigue.

4.6 Hazards in the office
4.7 VDUs

4.7.3 Design of workstations

Badly-designed workstations are the most likely cause of aches and pains. Check the following:

- Sufficient space on the worktop, with document holders if required;
- The worktop is at the right height;
- The printer is at the right height;
- The chair is comfortable and adjustable for height and angle;
- Lighting is sufficient to illuminate surfaces from which work is being copied;
- Lighting should not be directed straight onto the screen whether it is sunlight or artificial light – it can cause glare;
- Ambient lighting should not be too harsh;
- Daylight needs extra directional lighting for dull days and blinds for very sunny days;
- A comfortable working temperature is required;
- Use anti-static mats, sprays etc. *(See 3.2)* if necessary;
- A pleasing decor is helpful – if working towards a wall, make sure you look at something unobtrusive and restful;
- Do not work facing a window;
- Make sure you sit up straight with your back supported and with your hands at the right angle to the keyboard;
- Adjust the brightness of the screen to suit your requirements.

This section is not intended to be a complete or authoritative statement of the law, nor is it intended to be a substitute for taking legal advice on actual legal problems.

If a legal problem arises the person concerned is advised to go to a solicitor, legal advice or law centre or a Citizens Advice Bureau.

The addresses of local advice centres or CABx can be found in local telephone directories. Addresses of local solicitors and the types of work they do are listed in the Solicitors' Regional Directory which is available in public libraries.

5.1 ACAS

ACAS is the abbreviation for the Advisory, Conciliation and Arbitration Service *(for address see 12.12)*. This organisation's function is to promote the improvement of industrial relations. It issues Codes of Practice on good employment practices.

5.2 Data Protection Act 1984

This Act is designed to give individuals some protection from the effects of others holding computerised information about them.

Anyone collecting, using or storing personal information on a computer is affected by the Data Protection Act (DPA) except those who are specifically exempted.

If the data is held solely for purposes listed in (*a*)–(*d*) below then the data user does not have to register with the Data Protection Registry, nor allow others access to the information.

(*a*)   calculating pay or pensions
(*b*)   keeping accounts for a business
(*c*)   keeping records of transactions in order to make or request payment
(*d*)   keeping records of transactions in order to make financial or management forecasts

Data gained and used for any of these purposes must not be used in any other way. If it is used for a different purpose then the data user must register with the D. P. Registry *(for address see 12.12)*. A data user who does not have to register is only allowed to reveal the information to people such as accountants or auditors.

To make an application to be registered a business has to supply the following information:

5.1 ACAS
5.2 Data Protection Act 1984
5.3 Employment legislation

- the name and address of the data user
- a description of the data used and the reason for needing it
- a description of the sources of information
- a description of anyone who is likely to be given access to the data
- one or more addresses to which requests for access to the data can be sent

An entry on the register is intended to be an accurate description of who holds what data, why, and who is allowed access to it.

Therefore, if you are a registered data user and you want to use the information for a purpose you did not state on the entry, you must apply to have the entry changed. The same applies if you want to reveal the information to someone you did not mention on the entry.

A 'subject' of the data is the person whom the data is about. A data user holds information about subjects. Subjects have certain rights of access to the information.

If a subject asks, in writing, for a copy of the information held about him or her and pays the appropriate fee he or she is entitled to the copy within 40 days.

The police, tax authorities and some government departments do not have to reveal their information to the subject.

5.3 Employment legislation

Information on employment rights can be found in leaflets issued by the Information Branch of the Department of Employment *(see 12.12 for address)*. There are also a number of books on employment rights available, including the *Incomes Data Services Employment Law Handbooks* (published by Unwin) and a series called *Law at Work* (published by Sweet & Maxwell).

The laws about employment rights use the words 'full-time' and 'part-time' differently from the way these words are normally used. In law a full-time worker is someone who usually works 16 hours or more per week. A part-time worker is someone who works 8 or more hours but less than 16 hours per week. In this section the words are used following the legal definitions.

5.3.1 Dismissal

A full-time worker who has worked for 26 weeks or more must be given written reasons for his or her dismissal within 14 days of asking for them. A part-time worker has that right only after 5 years' work. **Wrongful dismissal** and **unfair dismissal** are not the same and claims relating to them are brought in different courts.

Wrongful dismissal This is where an employee is sacked in a way that breaks the terms of the contract. One of the terms of a contract of employment is how much notice the employee is entitled to. So if the employer gives the right amount of notice and follows the proper procedure the dismissal cannot be wrongful (but it may be unfair – *see below*).

For example, an employee who is entitled to 1 month's notice but is sacked on the spot may be able to claim wrongful dismissal. He or she would take the claim to the County Court. If the claim is successful the compensation will only be the pay the employee would have got if he or she had been given the right amount of notice; it will not include getting the job back.

However, if the employee in the example above had seriously broken the contract *first*, (e.g. by stealing) then the court may say the employer was entitled to dismiss without giving the proper notice.

Unfair dismissal If someone wants to bring a claim of unfair dismissal on the grounds of racial or sex discrimination it does not matter how many hours per week or for how long he or she had worked. (*See Race Relations Act, 5.4.3 and Sex Discrimination Acts 5.4.4.*)

A full-time worker may bring a claim for unfair dismissal only if he or she has been employed for at least 2 years by the same employer. A part-time worker may bring a claim after working for at least 5 years for the same employer.

A claim for unfair dismissal must be put before an Industrial Tribunal within 3 months of the end of the job.

In deciding whether or not a dismissal is unfair a Tribunal will look at the way in which the sacking was done as well as the reasons for it to see if the employer has been reasonable and fair.

Generally speaking, to defend an unfair dismissal claim an

employer has to show that there was a good enough reason for sacking the employee. This reason must be related to the employee's conduct, qualifications or competence. Alternatively the employer can plead that it was a redundancy situation.

> **5.3** Employment legislation

Constructive unfair dismissal   This is where an employee resigns because he or she feels that the situation at work has been made intolerable by the employer (*see e.g.* **4.5** *Harassment*). In other words, the employer has behaved in such a way as to break the contract of employment. This part of the law is aimed at employers who try and make people leave instead of sacking them directly.

Part-time workers   If the employer needs a full-time worker instead of a part-time worker he or she must first consult the part-time employee to see if that employee could do the job.

5.3.2   Maternity rights

(Although some employers may give fathers similar benefits there are no generally applicable paternity rights under English law.)

Ante-natal leave   Any pregnant woman, no matter what hours she works nor how long she has worked for the employer, is entitled to reasonable time off for going to ante-natal classes or doctor's appointments. She is also entitled to be paid for that time off.

Statutory Maternity Pay (SMP)   This replaces Maternity Pay and Maternity Allowance. To qualify for SMP an employee must have been employed for at least 26 weeks by the 15th week before the week in which the baby is due. An employee who does not qualify for SMP can apply for Maternity Allowance.

SMP is paid at two different rates. The higher rate is 90% of average weekly earnings. A full-time employee must have worked for the same employer for at least 2 years (5 years if part-time) to qualify for the higher rate. This is paid for the first 6 weeks of absence. If a woman is not eligible for the higher rate she is paid at the lower rate.

SMP is paid for a maximum of 18 weeks. After the first 6 weeks it is paid at the lower rate. There is a certain amount of flexibility as to when it starts to be paid. The employee can choose to start the 18 weeks' payment any time from the 11th week before the week in which the baby is due but, if she is to receive the full 18 weeks, she must start to receive SMP by the 6th week before the expected week of birth.

A further condition of receiving SMP is that the employee *must* tell the employer of her intention to stop work at least 21 days in advance, or as soon as is reasonably practicable.

The details of the SMP scheme are set out in the 'Employer's Guide to SMP' which is available from the DHSS.

Return to work   A full-time employee who has worked for the same employer for at least 2 years by the 11th week before the baby is due has a statutory right to return to work. She can exercise this right at any time within 29 weeks of the week of the birth. The terms and conditions of employment to which the woman returns must be no worse than they would have been if she had not been absent. The employee must notify the employer of her intention to return on a certain date at least 21 days in advance.

5.3.3   Notice

The employee's right to notice   An individual contract may say how much notice the employee is entitled to. If the contract does not specify the amount of notice the employee has the rights given by the law as stated below.

A full-time worker who has completed a month's work is entitled to 1 week's notice. After 2 years a full-time worker is entitled to 1 week's notice for every full year worked.

For example, a full-time worker who has been with the firm for 18 months only has a right to 1 week's notice (unless the contract specifies more). 6 months later she or he is entitled to 2 weeks' notice and to add a week for every year after that.

The maximum notice is 12 weeks except where an individual contract gives more.

Part-time workers are only entitled to 1 week's notice after 5 years' employment with the same employer. After 5 years they can add a week for every complete year worked.

The employer's right to notice   An individual contract may say how much notice an employee has to give of leaving a job. If it does not and the employee has been working for the same firm for 1 month or more he or she must give at least 1 week's notice.

5.3.4   Pay statement *(See also 7.10.1)*

A full-time worker is automatically entitled to an itemised pay statement. A part-time worker only has this right after 5 years' work.

An itemised statement should show:

- the gross pay;
- the amounts of any variable or fixed deductions and why they are made;
- the net amount payable;
- where a wage/salary is paid in different ways the statement must show the amount and method of each part-payment.

5.3.5 Redundancy

A redundancy situation is where the survival of the business means there must be a reduction in the number of employees.

A full-time worker is entitled to redundancy pay after 2 years' work. A part-time worker has the same right after 5 years. A worker is not entitled to redundancy pay if he or she is of retirement age.

With the right to redundancy pay comes the right to reasonable time off with pay to look for work once notice of redundancy has been given.

5.3.6 Statutory Sick Pay

Employers may make their own arrangements for paying people who are off sick (*see 1.5.6*). Statutory Sick Pay (SSP) is a scheme financed by the DHSS and administered by the employer to ensure a minimum payment to someone who falls ill. The employer makes the payments and then claims the money back from the DHSS. Self-employed people do not qualify for SSP.

For anything up to 28 weeks of sickness the employee may be entitled to SSP. If, for all or part of that time, she or he is not entitled to SSP then sickness benefit may be payable instead, depending on the National Insurance contributions that have been made.

The amount of SSP paid depends on the employee's average weekly earnings before the illness started. It is taxable and NI contributions continue to be paid from it.

After this, if the employee is still ill she or he moves on to Invalidity Benefit which is made up of Invalidity Pension (again, dependent on NI contributions) and Invalidity Allowance.

Further details can be found in a leaflet available from the DHSS called *Employer's guide to SSP*.

If the Sickness Benefit or Invalidity Benefit falls below a certain amount the employee can top it up by applying for Supplementary Benefit.

5.3.7   Statement of the terms of the contract

This is known as a 'Section One Statement'.

A full-time worker is entitled to receive and keep a written statement of the terms and conditions of the contract after 13 weeks' work. A part-time worker is entitled to this after 5 years and 13 weeks.

A Section One Statement should show:

- the names of the employer and the employee;
- the date when the job began;
- the scale/rate of pay;
- whether payment is made weekly, monthly etc.;
- the hours to be worked;
- the holiday entitlement, including public holidays and holiday pay;
- the terms for absence due to sickness, including sick pay arrangements;
- the terms of a pension scheme (if relevant);
- the length of notice to which an employee is entitled and the amount she or he must give of leaving;
- the job title;
- the disciplinary rules (or indicate where the employee can find them);
- the grievance procedure (how to make a complaint).

If the terms of employment change the employer should make a written statement of the changes available to the employee within 1 month.

5.3.8   Trade Unions

Every employee has a right to, or not to, join a Union as she or he chooses.

All workers have the right not to have action taken against them for Trade Union membership or activities.

5.4   Equal opportunities legislation

The Equal Opportunities Commission issues leaflets on equality and employment rights. *(For the address see 12.12.)*

5.4.1 Disabled Persons (Employment) Act 1944

A person can register as disabled if his or her condition is likely to last for 12 calendar months or more from the date of registration.

An employer who employs 20 people

5.3 Employment legislation
5.4 Equal opportunities

or more has a duty to employ a minimum quota of Registered Disabled People (RDP's). The usual quota is 3% of the workforce. Some trades and industries may have a different quota specified by the Secretary of State for Employment.

If an employer is not employing the required quota of Registered Disabled People he or she can be referred to the district advisory committee.

If an employer is not fulfilling the required quota there is *no* obligation to sack people who are not registered as disabled in order to take on someone who is. However, when a vacancy occurs the employer is obliged to consider someone who is a Registered Disabled Person.

The Disabled Persons (Employment) Act 1958 states that a Registered Disabled Person is entitled to have his or her name removed from the register on making an application.

There is a Code of Good Practice on the Employment of Disabled People available from the Manpower Services Commission *(for address see 12.12)*.

5.4.2 Equal Pay Act 1970

This Act states that if a woman is doing 'like work' with a man employed by the same employer the woman's contract should be no worse than the man's. In other words, the woman must be paid at the same rate and receive the same benefits as the man. If the woman's contract is worse the employer must improve it until it is equal to the man's contract. The employer is not allowed to downgrade the man's contract instead.

'Like work' means work that is rated as equal in terms of the demands made upon the worker (for instance in terms of the effort, skill and decision-making required). It is a way of saying that men and women should be paid equally for work of *equal value*. The comparison does not have to be between a man and a woman doing exactly the same work.

To justify a difference in the rate of pay an employer must be able to point to a 'material factor'. The difference in sex does not count as a 'material factor'.

Claims against employers made under this Act are brought before an Industrial Tribunal.

5.4.3 Race Relations Act 1976

This Act states that it is illegal to discriminate on racial grounds in the field of employment. 'Racial grounds' here means colour, race, nationality or ethnic or national origins.

Discrimination can be *direct* or *indirect*.

Direct discrimination is quite straightforward. It is defined as treating someone less favourably than others on racial grounds (or because of their sex – see *Sex Discrimination Acts below 5.4.4*).

Indirect discrimination works like this:

If, for example, an employer decides to advertise a vacancy for a store detective and, in the advert, says all applicants must be at least 5'10" the employer must be able to give a genuine, valid reason for the height requirement. If no valid reason could be given then it would be a case of indirect discrimination because fewer women than men would be able to meet the requirement.

An example of a requirement that would discriminate against Sikh men is a rule saying all porters must wear a peaked cap. However, a rule that all people working on a building site must wear a hard hat is not illegal. It would be discriminatory against Sikh men but is not illegal because there is a valid reason, *not* related to race, for making the rule, i.e. safety.

This Act makes it illegal to discriminate in recruitment procedures, in the provision of promotion or training opportunities, or of other benefits or facilities.

A complaint of racial discrimination should be made to an Industrial Tribunal within 3 months of the act complained of. *(See 12.12 for the address of the Commission for Racial Equality.)*

5.4.4 Sex Discrimination Acts 1975 and 1986

For an explanation of the meaning of direct and indirect discrimination see under *Race Relations Act* above.

This Act states that it is illegal to discriminate against someone on grounds of his or her sex in the field of employment.

It is also illegal to discriminate against married persons, directly or indirectly, because they are married.

The specific question of discrimination in rates of pay is dealt with by the Equal Pay Act 1970 (*see 5.4.2 above*). The Sex Discrimination

Act 1975 deals with discrimination in recruitment procedures, training and promotion opportunities. It used to apply only to businesses of a certain minimum size but the 1986 Act says that it applies to all business employers.

5.4 Equal opportunities
5.5 Health and Safety at Work

The SDA 1986 also makes it illegal to treat women and men unequally on the basis of age. This means that the retirement age must be the same for women and men who work for the same employer.

A claim of sex discrimination must be put before an Industrial Tribunal. *(See **12.12** for the address of the Equal Opportunities Commission.)*

5.5   Health and Safety at Work etc Act 1974

Employers' duties   This Act states that employers have a general duty to ensure, within reason, the health, safety and welfare at work of all their employees. This duty covers the provision of:

– safe machinery and systems
– safe means of handling, storing and transporting things
– appropriate training, instruction, information and supervision
– a safe place of work
– safe means of access to and from that place of work

Employers have a duty to produce a written statement of their general policy with regard to employees' health and safety, and of the ways they intend to carry out that policy. They should also bring this statement to the attention of all their employees.

If there are Safety Representatives appointed by the Trade Union employers must consult them about arrangements to be made and about checking the effectiveness of those arrangements.

Employers are not allowed to charge an employee for anything done or provided in the course of fulfilling the legal duties arising out of this Act.

Employers and self-employed people must ensure that people on their premises but not employed by them (e.g. customers, visiting engineers) are not exposed to health or safety risks.

A record must be kept of all accidents *(see **4.1**)*.

Employees' duties   Employees have a general duty to take reasonable care for their own health and safety and that of others at the place of work. They must co-operate with the employer in the implementation of health and safety policies.

5.5.1 Employer's Liability (Defective Equipment) Act 1969

'Equipment', in this Act, means plant, machinery, vehicles, aircraft and clothing.

If an employee is injured at work because of a defect in the equipment provided by the employer, and the defect was caused by a third party (such as a manufacturer) the employer is liable for the injury on the grounds of negligence.

An employer cannot deny his or her liability under this Act.

If the employee is partly responsible for the accident that fact will be taken into account by a court when assessing a claim for damages.

5.6 Insurance

5.6.1 Employer's Liability (Compulsory Insurance) Act 1969

In the same way as a car owner must be insured, so an employer must be insured against accidents to employees or visitors.

An employer must display copies of the certificate of insurance at each place of business where someone is employed. The certificate displayed must not be out of date. There must be enough copies in accessible places for all employees to be able to see and read one.

If the employees are relations of the employer (as defined by the Act) then insurance is not essential.

Certain employers do not have to comply with this Act. Such employers include local authorities, police authorities and nationalised industries.

5.7 Offices, Shops and Railway Premises Act 1963

This Act does not apply to premises where only outworkers or the employer's relatives work. It also does not apply to premises where employees normally work for 21 hours or less per week.

Premises must be kept clean.

Floors, stairs, corridors etc. must be free from obstructions and slippery substances.

There must be:

- suitable lighting
- sufficient toilets and washing facilities
- space for clothes not worn while working
- reasonable facilities for sitting down, where appropriate
- adequate ventilation

5.5 Health and Safety at Work
5.6 Insurance
5.7 Offices Act 1963

The premises must be maintained at a reasonable temperature. (16°C is the usual minimum temperature.)

The premises must not be overcrowded (bearing in mind the space taken up by equipment).

Dangerous parts of machinery must be securely fenced. People under 18 must not be asked to clean dangerous machinery. People required to operate dangerous machines must be fully instructed and adequately trained or supervised.

No one should be asked to lift or move a load so heavy that it is likely to injure them.

In shops there must be suitable separate eating facilities.

6.1 Business meeting terms

6.1.1 Definitions and expressions

Abstentions   Number of people abstaining when a vote is taken. Number of abstentions is usually recorded in the Minutes.

Address the Chair   Speak to and through the Chair, so that order is maintained.

Adjourn   Break off for later resumption.

Adopt   To agree the content of, e.g. adopt a report, the accounts, etc.

Agenda   List of matters to be discussed. *(See 6.2.2)*

Amendment   An amendment to a formal 'motion'. An amendment should be voted on *before* the motion is voted on.

AOB   Any Other Business – last item on Agenda, but often omitted at very large and formal meetings.

Apology   A formal apology for absence sent in by letter, telephone, telemessage, etc.

Ballot Papers   Official forms for registering votes.

Carried over   Not decided – carried over to the next meeting.

Casting Vote   A vote used by the Chair to tip the balance if voting is equal.

The Chair's Notes   The Chair's personal guide to the meeting. *(See 6.2.3)*

Consensus   The agreed view of the meeting.

Co-opted member   Someone not elected but asked to attend the meeting, often to give specialist advice or replace a member who has unexpectedly retired, etc.

Ex officio   By virtue of the office held, e.g. a Treasurer is automatically a member of a committee because he or she is Treasurer.

For and against   Votes for or against a motion.

Has the floor   Is entitled to speak without interruption.

In attendance   Someone attending the meeting who is not actually part of the meeting e.g. an observer or officer.

In camera   In secret – observers, reporters etc. are excluded.

In the Chair   In charge of the meeting.

Intra vires Is within the powers – it can be done constitutionally.
Invitation Formal invitation (sometimes summons) to attend the meeting. *(See 6.2.1)*

6.1 Business meeting terms

Matters Arising Matters for discussion which arise out of the Minutes of the previous meeting.
Majority Report A report, or decision, agreed to by the majority of the members – not a consensus.
Minority Report A report etc. agreed to by a minority of the members, but substantial enough to be worthy of note – not a consensus.
Minutes Detailed record of the meeting (from 'minutiae' – details). Copy signed by the Chair is the official record. *(See 6.2.4)*
Motion A formal, carefully-worded proposition, which must be precisely recorded in the Minutes.
Move Formally propose (a motion, etc.).

Nem con Passed with no-one against (unanimous).
No confidence No confidence in the 'leaders', usually on a serious subject; if a motion of 'no confidence' is put and voted for, the Chair would normally resign.
Nomination Form Form used to nominate candidates when an election is to be held. *(See 6.2.5)*
Note Members of the meeting formally take note that something has happened (e.g. what another committee has said on the subject).
Notice of Meeting Formal invitation to attend meeting. *(See 6.2.1)*
Notice of Motion A notice that a motion will be included in the business of the meeting. Required to be given well in advance with the motion set down in precise terms.

Off the record Not to be recorded or minuted.
On the table A proposition or formal motion has been moved and seconded and must be decided before the meeting can go on to the next item.

Point of order Query raised by a member of the meeting as to whether an occurrence is within the constitution or rules of the meeting.
Proposer Someone who formally proposes a motion or the adoption of the accounts, etc.

Proposition   A proposal – not as formal as a 'motion'.
Proxy   Someone who can vote on behalf of another.

Quorum   The number of members who must be present before the meeting can 'legally' start. This varies according to the nature of the meeting and is often laid down in the constitution. A 'quorate' meeting has a quorum.

Receive   Formally to receive, perhaps adopt, a report etc.
Resolution   Akin to a proposition.
Rider   An additional note which qualifies in some way the previous note or statement.
Right of reply   The right to reply to a critical comment or accusation.

Seconder   Someone who formally seconds (supports) the proposer of a motion, etc.
Sine die   without setting a new date – a meeting can be adjourned sine die.

Tabled   Papers, discussion documents etc., which are introduced (put on the table) at the meeting – not sent out beforehand.
Through the Chair   Members speak to each other 'through' the Chair, so that order is maintained *(see 'Address the Chair')*.

Ultra vires   Outside the terms or powers of the meeting.
Unanimous   Nobody against (nem con).

Voting rights   Some members may have the right to vote on a motion and others (e.g. observers) may not.

6.1.2   People

President   The person who is the 'head' of the society, organisation etc. (head of a company in the USA) and who 'presides' over or takes the Chair at large meetings, e.g. an AGM.
Vice President   A person who can deputise for the President; this is sometimes an honorary position granted for service to the organisation.
Chairman/Chairwoman/Chairperson/The Chair   The person in charge of the meeting.
Deputy Chair/Vice Chair   Deputy to the Chair.
Secretary   The person in charge of the administration of the meeting, responsible for the provision of documents, the taking of Minutes etc.

Minutes Secretary Someone whose only job is to take the Minutes and is not part of the meeting itself.

Treasurer The person in charge of the finances.

Member Someone elected, appointed or invited to attend a meeting, usually with voting rights.

> **6.1** Business meeting terms

Representative Someone who represents others (usually elected).

Delegate Someone who attends on behalf of another (usually appointed).

Officers Those who are concerned with administering the meeting (secretary, treasurer etc.).

Observers People invited to sit in and observe a meeting – usually with no voting rights and sometimes without the right to say anything.

6.1.3 Types of meeting

Annual General Meeting (AGM) A formal meeting of all members of a company, society etc. held once a year to report progress, elect officers etc.

Committee A small body of members (usually elected) who meet regularly and generally run the organisation *or* people invited to join an organisation to oversee a specific project etc.

Conference A large meeting of representatives or private individuals who meet to confer on a given theme; there is often an element of learning involved, with visiting speakers etc.

Congress A meeting of similar organisations (e.g. the Trades Union Congress).

Extraordinary General Meeting A meeting of all members called in addition to the AGM when some urgent and often unexpected matter needs to be discussed by all members.

Sub-Committee A very small number of people, usually appointed by a Committee, to study, organise and report on a very specific subject (e.g. a Catering Sub-Committee).

Teleconference A meeting of people in different locations by telephone or closed-circuit television; not necessarily a large meeting. Chairing this type of meeting calls for additional skills in controlling people who are distant from one another and, over the telephone, cannot see each other. *(See 3.14)*

Working Party Very similar to a sub-committee – usually not more than about six people who work on a very specific project or topic.

6.2   Formal meeting documents

6.2.1   *Invitation to Meeting*

This is a formal invitation to attend a meeting, and may be in the form of a Summons, a Notice of Meeting, an Invitation or other similar document; must be sent out in good time to allow members to prepare for the meeting. Time of sending is sometimes set down in the constitution.

The invitation should contain:

- Title of meeting (Committee Meeting, Annual General Meeting etc.);
- Date, time, place and room name or number;
- Response required (tear-off slip confirming attendance etc.);
- Emergency telephone number for latecomers.

Send directions and/or map as necessary.

The Notice might look like this:

Date

N O T I C E
of the
ANNUAL GENERAL MEETING
of the
[Name of Organisation]

NOTICE is hereby given that the Annual General Meeting of the [name] will be held on [Date] at [Time] at [Venue].

Please indicate whether or not you are able to attend by completing the form below and returning it to me not later than [Date].

Secretary.

[Reply slip]

Documents to accompany invitation:

- Agenda *(See 6.2.2)*
- Minutes of previous meeting *(See 6.2.4)*
- Nomination forms (for AGM elections etc.) if required *(See 6.2.5)*
- Copies of papers for discussion at meeting.

6.2.2 Agenda

This is the list of matters to be discussed at the meeting and should be sent out with the Invitation to allow members adequate preparation time. A typical layout is as follows:

6.2 Formal meeting documents

[Name of Organisation]
[Title of Meeting]
[Time, Date and Place of Meeting]

AGENDA

1 Apologies for absence
2 Minutes of previous meeting
3 Matters arising
4 [Matters for discussion, as agreed with Chair]
5 [etc.]
6 [etc.]
7 Date(s) of next meeting(s)
8 Any Other Business

6.2.3 The Chair's Notes

These are personal notes usually prepared by the Secretary to help the Chair conduct the meeting without leaving out important points.

A typical layout might be:

[Name of Organisation]
[Title of Meeting]
[Time, Date and Place of Meeting]

NOTES

1 Apologies   Mr A Jones
              Miss B Smith
2 Minutes   Amendment sent in by Miss Smith
3 Matters   Report on builder's comments re drains.

6.2.4 Minutes

The Minutes are the formal record of the meeting. The Secretary must take personal notes during the meeting, following the Agenda and all items discussed, and write up the Minutes as soon after the meeting as possible. The Minutes are often agreed with the Chair before they are circulated to members.

The Minutes are not adopted as the formal record until they have been agreed and signed by the Chair at the next meeting. Usually Minutes are sent out with the Invitation *(See 6.2.1)* so that members can study them beforehand. Amendments to the Minutes can be made at the next meeting with the agreement of the members; any hand-written amendments should be initialled by the Chair.

A typical layout is:

MINUTES
of the [Title of Meeting]
held on [Date] at [Venue] at [Time]

Present: Mr K Abado (in the Chair)
                  [List of other members present]
In attendance: [Observers, officers etc. who are not an official
                  part of the meeting *(See 6.1.2)*]

1 Apologies for absence
Apologies for absence were received from Mr A Jones and Miss B Smith.

2 Minutes of previous meeting
The Minutes of the meeting of [date] were taken as read, confirmed and signed.

3 Matters arising

3.1 Drains
The Chair reported that the builder had inspected the drains and found a crack in the pipe underneath the kitchen floor; an estimate of costs for the repair would be submitted at the next meeting.

[. . . and so on down the Agenda.]

The Minutes usually end with a formal sentence such as:

'There being no further business, the Chair closed the meeting at (time).'

Space should then be left for the signature of the Chair and the date on which the Minutes were signed.

Signed . . . . (Chair)

Date . . . .

If you are taking over the position of Secretary to a meeting, there will usually be a layout of the Minutes for you to follow.

6.2.5 *Nomination Form*
This is usually sent out with the Invitation *(See 6.2.1)* when one of the items on the Agenda is the election of officers. The form should be drawn up in accordance with the constitution of the organisation; look for a precedent in the file, but a typical layout might be:

[Title of organisation]		
NOMINATION FORM		
Office	*Present Holder*	*Member Nominated*
Chair	Mr P Carter	. . . .
Proposed by: Name	*Signature*	
Seconded by: Name	*Signature*	

6.3 Preparation and follow-up

6.3.1 *Before the day*

  – Book room – date, time and duration;
  – Find out names of people attending;
  – Send out meeting documents in good time *(See 6.2)*;
  – Order refreshments;
  – Inform reception, car park attendant, etc.;
  – Check visual aids (screen, OHP, video, flipboard) etc. available *(See 2.14)*;
  – Prepare The Chair's Notes (if required) *(See 6.2.3)*;
  – List apologies for absence;
  – Prepare nameplates (if required);
  – Check arrangements for room and refreshments.

6.3.2 On the day – before the meeting

- Check room is ready – correct numbers of tables and chairs; heating, lighting and ventilation; ashtrays, blank paper and pencils, nameplates, gavel etc.; somewhere to put coats, umbrellas and briefcases;
- Assemble visual aids (video, screen and OHP etc.) and check that they are working;
- Check refreshment times and refreshment arrangements;
- Arrange side table for coffee, tea etc. (borrow one if necessary);
- Have spare copies of Agenda, Minutes and other relevant papers;
- Have background information (previous correspondence etc.) available;
- Have pen for Chair to sign Minutes;
- Have Chair's notes ready (if required);
- Stop all telephone calls to room and make arrangements for messages to be left.

6.3.3 On the day – during and after the meeting

- Help latecomers settle discreetly (take coat etc.) or make arrangements if you are taking the Minutes;
- Feed documents to Chair as required;
- Take Minutes (if required) *(See 6.2.4)*;
- Ensure ashtrays emptied, coffee cups etc. cleared away during breaks;
- Take care of confidential documents;
- Check nothing is left behind;
- Return borrowed visual aids, table etc.;
- Thank refreshment staff.

6.3.4 After the meeting

- Prepare Minutes (if required) and check with Chair;
- Circulate Minutes.

7.1 Arithmetical calculations

7.1.1 Currency conversion
For currency denominations see 12.4.

Banks and other organisations who exchange currencies usually set out the exchange rates something like this:

	We buy	*We sell*
Swiss Fr.	2.41	2.24
Comm.	2%	1%

If you want to buy £200 worth of Swiss Francs the bank will sell them to you at an exchange rate of 2.24. This means that for every £1 the bank will give you 2.24 Swiss Francs.

Therefore to calculate how many Swiss Francs you can buy for £200 you simply have to multiply 2.24 by 200:

$2.24 \times 200 = 448$ Swiss Francs

However, you have to remember to take off the commission so the final total of Swiss Francs will be

$448 - 4\ 48\ (1\%) = \mathbf{443.52SF}$

If, on return from the business trip, the traveller has 40 Swiss Francs left and wants to change them back into sterling, then the bank will buy the foreign currency back at the rate of 2.41. This means that for every 2.41 Swiss Francs you exchange you will receive £1.

To calculate this you divide the number of Francs by the exchange rate:

$40 \div 2.41 = 16.60$

Again, you have to take off the commission for the exchange service:

$16.60 - 0.33\ (2\%) = \mathbf{£16.27}$

(Some organisations charge a fixed rate for exchanging currencies rather than a percentage, and most will only change notes, not coins.)

7.1.2 Discounts

Example (*i*) '£5 off every item priced at £100 or more'
If a customer then puts in an order for an item worth £245 and the discount applies it is a simple matter of taking £5 off the total price.

£245 − £5 = **£240**

Example (*ii*) '£15 off for every complete £150 spent'
The customer orders goods worth £309.

Divide the total of the order (£309) by the qualifying amount specified (£150).

309 ÷ 150 = 2.06

Thus the customer is spending 2 × 150, but not as much as 3 × 150, and so is entitled to 2 × £15 as a discount.

2 × £15 = £30

You then subtract the discount from the original total to give the amount the customer will pay.

£309 − £30 = **£279**

Example (*iii*) The discount may be expressed as a percentage: '5% discount on every order over £1000'

A customer who orders goods worth £900 will not be entitled to any discount because £1000 worth of goods must be ordered to qualify for the discount.

If a customer orders goods worth £1567 the discount will be worked out like this *(see **7.1.3** below for percentages)*.

5% of £1567 = £78.35

Then subtract the amount of the discount from the original price.

£1567 − £78.35 = **£1488.65**

7.1.3 Percentages
Example 15% of £17.23 = ?
Step one: Multiply 17.23 by 15.

17.23 × 15 = 258.45

Step two: Divide the total of that sum by 100.

258.45 ÷ 100 = **2.5845**

For everyday use it is not necessary to know more than two figures after the decimal point. If the 3rd figure is 5 or more then add 1 on to the 2nd figure after the decimal point (e.g. if the total were 2.5854 then add 1 to the 8 and drop the last two figures: 2.59.) This is 'rounding up'. If the 3rd figure after the

> **7.1** Arithmetical calculations

decimal point is a 4 or less then just drop the last two figures. So, in the example above 2.5845 would be treated as 2.58.

Thus 15% of £17.23 = **£2.58**

7.1.4 VAT

VAT is currently charged at the rate of 15%. To add VAT on to a total is always simply a matter of adding on 15% (*see 7.1.3 above*).

However, to subtract VAT is not so simple – it is not a matter of deducting 15% of the total.

For example, 15% of £100 is £15, giving a total of £115, but 15% of £115 is £17.25 – *not* the amount that was added on as VAT in the first place.

The formula for finding out how much of a total is VAT is to divide the total by 23 and multiply the result by 3. If the tax rate is different then the fraction will change too. The local VAT inspector can give you the new formula. The following examples are with VAT at 15%.

Example (*i*) If you have a total (e.g. £115) and you want to find out how much of that total is VAT then:
Step one: Divide the number by 23

$115 \div 23 = 5$

Step two: Multiply that new figure by 3

$5 \times 3 = 15$

Thus the VAT paid in a price of £115 is **£15**.
The net price without VAT is found by subtracting the VAT figure from the original total.

$£115 - £15 = £100$

Example (*ii*) £375.41 is the total amount paid.
Step one: Divide by 23

$375.41 \div 23 = 16.32$ (to 2 figures after the decimal point)

Step two: Multiply by 3

16.32 × 3 = **48.96**

Of the £375.41, £48.96 is VAT. Thus the net figure of the price before VAT is:

375.41 − 48.96 = **£326.45**

(See 7.9 for other information on VAT.)

7.2 Banking

All cheques, cheque books, paying-in books and bank statements should be kept securely.

7.2.1 Cheques

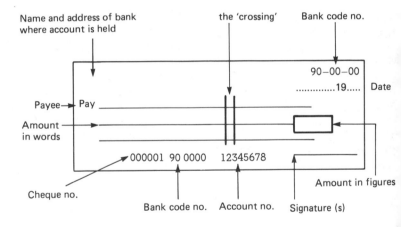

The *drawer* is the person in whose name the account is held.

The *payee* is the person who is being paid.

The amount on a cheque must be the same in words and in figures.

Any corrections should be initialled by the drawer. No alterations can be made to cheques printed by a cheque-writing machine.

There should be no gaps where someone could add in a figure or change the name of the payee.

A *cheque signer* is a metal plate which can be applied to produce the signature of the person authorised to sign cheques. The plate must be removed when it is not in use. The machine is lockable and has a numbering device so the number of cheques signed is recorded.

7.1 Arithmetical calculations
7.2 Banking

The *crossing* can be general or special. A general crossing is where the two vertical lines are left blank or the words '& Co.' are written between them. If a cheque is crossed like this it can only be paid into a bank account and cannot be cashed.

A special crossing is where the name of an account is written between the vertical lines ensuring that the cheque can only be paid into that specific account.

A cheque can be *endorsed* by the payee signing it on the back. This has the effect of allowing someone else to pay the cheque into their bank account.

A *dishonoured* cheque is one which the bank of the drawer refuses to pay because there are not enough funds in the account. The payee is notified when this occurs.

Stopping a cheque can be done by telephone and confirmed in writing. The bank will need to know the cheque number, the date of the cheque, the amount and the name of the payee. A fee may be charged for this service.

7.2.2 Paying-in
This is usually done on a paying-in book specific to one account. The information that must be filled in on the paying-in slip includes the name of the account holder (unless already printed), the date, the name of the person paying the money in, a breakdown of any cash and the details of any cheques.

7.2.3 Bank statement
Bank statements should be kept and each entry checked against the counterfoils.

Abbreviations which commonly appear on statements include:

CH   Charges/Commission
CT   Credit Transfer
DD   Direct Debit
IN   Interest

O/D   Overdrawn
SO   Standing Order

7.3   Banking services

Banker's Draft   This is a written order for payment which can be cashed by the bearer – it is not crossed like a cheque. It is cleared more quickly through the banking system than a cheque.

Bank Statement   This shows all transactions *(see 7.2.3)*. Sent weekly or monthly as requested.

Current account   is for day-to-day transactions. Most current accounts earn no interest. Cheque card and cheque books are provided for drawing on the account.

Credit Transfer   This is where a bank customer wishes to pay several bills at once. The customer sends a list to the bank giving the name, branch and account number of each creditor and the amount due to each one. Only one cheque for the total amount owed needs to be sent to the bank. The customer must check with the creditors that they will accept payment by this method. It is often used for paying employees.

Deposit account   This earns interest. Notice is usually required to make withdrawals.

Direct Debit   This is when the payee tells the bank how much is to be deducted from the drawer's account. The drawer's written agreement must be given first. The amount can be varied by the payee once the drawer has been notified.

Night Safe   This is used for lodging money and valuables with the bank outside banking hours. The customer has a lockable leather pouch and a key to the safe.

Open credit   This is an arrangement to cash cheques at a branch or bank other than where the account is held. It is a service available nationally or internationally.

Secure storage   This is a service for the safe keeping of documents and valuables.

Standing Order   This is when a specific sum is paid regularly to the same payee e.g. a subscription. Unlike a Direct Debit this amount cannot be varied by the payee.

SWIFT The Society for Worldwide Interbank Financial Telecommunication is a computer based network for the international exchange of banking information (payments, statements etc.).

Telegraphic Transfer TT is a system for making international payments by cable/telegraph. If using SWIFT they are sent as 'urgent SWIFT messages'.

(Travellers' cheques and foreign currency See 11.4.)

7.4 Credit cards

Any piece of plastic that is used to pay for purchases tends to be described as a credit card but not all plastic cards are credit cards in the strict sense of the term. These are the different types of card you might use.

7.4.1 Cash card

The holder of a cash card can withdraw money from the account at a cash dispenser both within and outside banking hours. A Personal Identification Number (PIN) is issued with the card and must be used when drawing money out. This number must not be disclosed to any unauthorised person. It is better not to write it down at all but to memorise it. The trick of writing it as if it were a phone number is well known to thieves.

7.4.2 Charge card

You can borrow money with a charge card, but only for a limited length of time as the account must be paid in full every month. The advantage of these cards, such as Diners or American Express, is that there is often no credit limit and interest is not charged so the borrowing facility is free. However, there is a yearly charge for 'membership'.

7.4.3 Cheque guarantee card

As the name implies, presentation of this card guarantees that the bank will honour the cheque. Cheque cards can only be used with cheques for £50 or less.

7.4.4   Credit card
Access and Visa are examples of credit cards in the strict sense of the term. When you present a credit card the bill is charged to the credit account. At the end of each month the credit company sends the holder a bill for the total amount outstanding. You do not have to pay off the whole account each month. Each statement of account will show the previous balance (how much is due from the month(s) before), the new balance (how much is now due) and the minimum payment that must be made. Interest is charged on the amount left unpaid and carried forward to the next month's account. Each card holder has a credit limit.

7.4.5   Debit card
This is the reverse of a credit card. The holder of the card pays a certain amount into the account and then presents the card, instead of cash, and the bill is debited from the total in the account. A debit card is used for the EFTPOS system *(see 7.4.6 below)*.

7.4.6   EFTPOS (Electronic Funds Transfer at Point of Sale)
In this sytem shops link up with banks or Building Societies so that when a customer reaches the till, instead of paying by cash, cheque or credit card, she or he presents a debit card and the total bill is automatically deducted from the account held with the bank or Building Society. For security the customer has a Personal Identification Number and the cashier is able to operate the sytem without knowing the PIN number or the amount held in the account.

7.5   Expenses
Certain expenditures made in the course of a job can be deducted from the employee's total income when it comes to assessing how much tax he or she has to pay. *(See 7.10.3.)* If a tax inspector so requests then an employer must fill in returns stating benefits paid or provided for employees.

7.5.1   Travel expenses
Expenses for travelling between work and home are not deductible, but the cost of travel between offices or sites for the one job is deductible. The travel must be necessary for the performance of the job but does not have to be made solely for that purpose. For example, if it is essential as part of your job that you go on a

business trip to another city then the cost of travelling is deductible even if you then combine it with another purpose not connected with the job.

7.5.2 Other expenses

In order to be deductible from total income any expenses which are not travel expenses must be incurred necessarily, wholly and exclusively in the performance of a job. For example the cost of a meal at work or a suit bought for work is *not* deductible because we have to eat and wear clothes anyway, but the cost of maintaining tools or special clothing required for work *is* deductible.

7.6 Pensions

The theory behind a pension system is that you pay in a small amount each week or month and receive a lump sum or a series of payments on retirement. It is a way of saving money while you are earning, in preparation for the time when you will no longer be earning.

State Pension Payment of National Insurance contributions goes towards a state pension. To receive the full pension you have to have paid a minimum amount each year in N.I. contributions for a certain number of years (at present 40).

Private pension To supplement the state pension most employers run their own pension fund for their employees. From April 1988 membership of a company scheme cannot be made compulsory, so you can 'contract out' if you do not want to participate in that particular fund. Other schemes do not automatically include everyone, in which case you 'contract in' if you wish to. Pension funds are either contributory or non-contributory, that is, the employee may or may not have to make payments into the scheme. This depends on the terms of the scheme.

If you leave a job where you contributed to a pension fund one of three options may be open to you.

(*a*) You leave the contributions in that fund and receive the pension due on them at retirement age. (The longer you worked there the larger the pension will be when it is paid.)

(*b*) You may be able to transfer your contributions to the pension fund of the next job. For example, pensions can be transferred between local authorities.

(c)   You may be able to cash in your contributions then and there. However, you should remember that tax relief is given on some pension contributions and therefore if you cash them in early you may have to pay the tax on them at that point.

7.7   Petty cash

To operate a petty cash system you will need:

– a lockable cash box
– petty cash vouchers (available at most stationers)
– a petty cash book

7.7.1   The Imprest system

The float is fixed at a certain amount for a certain period of time. The details of each expenditure must be written on a petty cash voucher. Examples of payments made from the petty cash might include stamps, reimbursement for petrol or fares, paying for tea or coffee. Any receipts should be attached to the relevant voucher.

Petty Cash Voucher

Folio 7		Date 26/10/8–
For what required	£	p
TRAIN FARE (RETURN TO LONDON)	1	40
REGISTERED LETTER	1	20
Signature	Passed by	

Note: Each item is shown separately. Each folio must be numbered and dated. The person being reimbursed must sign the voucher.

The amount shown on the vouchers and the remaining cash

should add up to the fixed amount of the float. For example, if the float is £30 and the vouchers show that £15 has been paid out there should be £15 cash in the box.

A petty cash book is kept to record all expenditure. Some firms prefer payments to be entered as soon as possible, others leave it until the float is renewed at the end of the fixed period. The entries in the book might be laid out like this:

7.7 Petty cash

Dr						Petty Cash					Cr
Receipts		Date	Details	Folio No.	Total		Postage	Travel	Station-ery	Sundries	
12	31	Oct 1	To balance b/d								
17	69	1	Cash								
		2	stamps	1	3	10	3 10				
		5	Taxi fare	2	3	80		3 80			
		8	Teabags	3	1	99				1 99	
		10	Petrol	4	10	00		10 00			
		10	Milk	3		48				48	
					19	37	3 10	13 80	—	—	2 47
		15	Balance c/d		11	63					
30	00				30	00					
11	63		To balance b/d								
19	37	16	Cash								

In this example, the accounting period is a fortnight and the float is £30. The total spent on travel, for instance, was £13.80. The cash

needed to make the float up to £30 at the end of the fortnight was
£19.37.

7.8   Security

In an office it is not only money and personal belongings that are at
risk but the equipment and documents. Here are some suggestions
for maintaining a good standard of security at your place of work:

- Keep offices and store rooms locked when no one is using them;
- Keep 'Confidential' documents in locked filing cabinets when
  not using them;
- Keep boxes of computer and word processor disks with confi-
  dential information locked;
- Make a note of how many keys are in circulation and who has
  them;
- Keep all money and banking books in a locked cupboard or safe;
- Keep lists of passwords for accessing computer files separate
  from the files.

7.9   VAT

To calculate VAT see 7.1.4.

Every VAT registered person who produces, sells or buys goods
or services pays VAT on the purchases and charges it on sales. Thus
the retailer may pay VAT on the goods bought from the wholesaler
but is able to pass it on to the consumer. The consumer cannot pass
the VAT on because he or she does not sell anything.

Every business with a turnover above a certain amount is liable to
register for VAT. Every registered business must complete a VAT
return for HM Customs and Excise at the end of every quarter as
requested.

A VAT return shows 'tax due'. This is the amount of VAT that
has been charged to other people on sales. The tax is due to HM
Customs and Excise. The return also shows 'tax deductible'. This is
the amount of VAT that the trader has already paid by buying other
goods and services.

If the tax due is greater than that already paid on purchases then
the trader owes the difference between the 'tax due' figure and the
'tax deductible' figure to HM Customs and Excise. Remittance for
this amount must be enclosed with the VAT return.

If the 'tax deductible' is more than the 'tax due' then there is a net amount owing to the trader from HM Customs and Excise.

All goods and services are VAT-able unless specifically exempted (like train fares) or zero-rated (like gas and electricity). For example a printing firm that prints posters, newspapers and books will charge VAT on the posters but not on the newspapers or books as they are zero-rated.

7.10 Wages, salaries and tax

'Wage' and 'salary' mean the same thing but usually 'wage' refers to a weekly payment and 'salary' to a monthly payment.

7.10.1 Pay statement
(See also 5.3.4)

A simple statement of pay may look like this:

Name A. Person		*Week Ending* 10th April 1987	
		Wage	£110.00
National Insurance	£9.92	*Overtime*	—
Tax	£20.10	*Gross Pay*	£110.00
Pension	£6.50		
		Less Total Deductions	£36.52
		Nett Pay	**£73.48**

Gross Pay is the amount after overtime and bonuses but before any deductions. Nett Pay is the amount actually received, after deductions have been made. National Insurance and Income Tax are statutory deductions that must be paid. The pension may be a voluntary deduction. Examples of other voluntary deductions include trade union dues, charity donations and company sports club subscriptions.

7.10.2 National Insurance
A percentage of all employees' salaries is deducted as National Insurance contributions. There is an upper limit on the amount that can be deducted. The employer also makes a contribution for each employee. The contribution is calculated in relation to the amount of the gross pay. The DHSS collects both the employer's contribution and the employee's contribution from the employer. The

Employer's Guide to National Insurance Contributions gives details of how to calculate the deductions and is available from the DHSS.

7.10.3   Income Tax

The scheme for employees' tax is the Pay As You Earn system (PAYE) (Schedule E). Everyone has a tax allowance which is an amount that can be earned in one tax year without paying any tax. The allowance for each person depends on various factors, such as marital status, and is allocated by the tax office. It is related to the PAYE code issued to all employees by the tax office. Anyone who does not have a code is charged tax at the emergency tax rate and any overpayment is repaid to that person when a code is issued.

There are different rates of tax for different salary brackets. Thus if, in one tax year (April 5th to April 4th) your earnings go over the maximum for taxing at the standard rate, part of your salary will be taxed at a higher rate.

Every employee is assigned to a tax office, not according to where he or she lives, but according to the location of the employer (Head Office if there is one). In case of any tax queries that tax office is the place to contact.

A P60 is a form issued to every employee at the end of the tax year which shows how much has been earned and how much tax paid in that year.

A P45 is a form issued when an employee leaves a job. It shows how much has been earned and paid in the tax year up to the end of that job. On starting a new job or signing on at the Unemployment Office the employee will need to produce the P45 so that she or he is taxed at the correct rate from the beginning.

If you are responsible for calculating the wages/salaries of the employees in your firm you will need to contact the relevant tax office to get a copy of the current rates and any advice on how to make the calculations.

There are two *main* types of structure: private business, including banks and insurance companies, and public service – the Civil Service, Local Authorities etc.

8.1 Private business structure

A typical private business structure for a limited company works like this:

Shareholders They own the business, by putting in money and having certain voting rights.

Chair(man) or President He/she is responsible to the Shareholders and the Board of Directors, with overall accountability for the business.

Managing Director/Chief Executive He/she is responsible to the Chairman and the Board of Directors for the general running of the business.

Board of Directors This is a body of people who may, or may not, be employees of the company, responsible for making general policy decisions. Some Directors are 'expert' in a particular field. Others may be part of a family business, with or without direct working responsibility in the company.

Company Secretary He/she serves the Board of Directors as administrator; sometimes legal adviser, constitutional adviser etc. to the company.

Executive Directors They are usually responsible for a specific aspect of the business, e.g.

- Sales
- Marketing
- Finance
- Personnel and Training
- Production/Operations
- Transport
- Information Services

Managers/Executives They could be Regional or Area Managers in large companies. Usually responsible to a certain Director for a specific area of work, e.g. Production Manager to Operations Director. Managers often have Assistant or Deputy Managers.

Department Managers/Supervisors/Foremen   These are heads of a section or department, e.g. Despatch Manager responsible to the Production Manager. This is a first-level management position, often with a Deputy.

Staff/Operatives   The people at the 'sharp' end who produce the goods or render the services.

A typical 'family tree' might look like the one on the opposite page.

8.2   Public service structure

This differs from organisation to organisation, but tends to work on 'grades'. A typical Civil Service grading system, starting with the lowest grade, is:

AA	Administrative Assistant
AO	Administrative Officer
EO	Executive Officer
HEO	Higher Executive Officer
SEO	Senior Executive Officer
	Principal
	Senior Principal (becoming rare)
	Assistant Secretary
	Under Secretary
	Permanent Secretary

Knowledge of this grading system, or its equivalent, can be very helpful when dealing with public bodies.

8.3   Units of business ownership

8.3.1   Sole trader
A sole trader is an individual working on his/her own account. The sole trader is personally liable for all debts and claims made against the business. Claims can be made against his/her estate on death.

8.3.2   Partnership
Profits and losses are shared among the partners. Partners are liable individually as well as jointly for all debts and claims against the

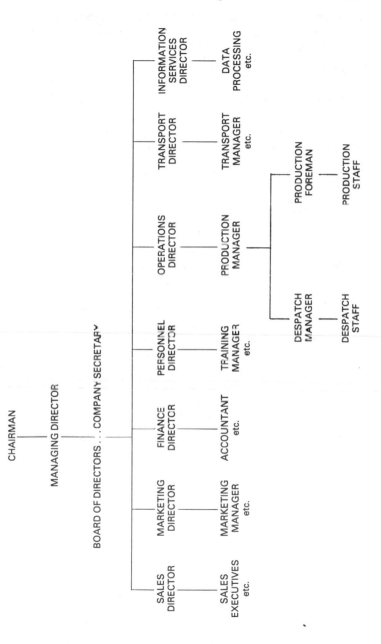

business, even though one partner may not know what another has done. If any of the partners resigns or dies, the partnership no longer exists and has to be re-formed if required. A Partnership Agreement setting out distribution of profits, how losses will be apportioned and what to do if a partner resigns or dies is desirable.

8.3.3   Limited liability company

Each individual invests a specified sum in shares issued by the company. Personal liability is limited to the nominal value of the shares held by the individual. The assets of the company belong to the company, and not to individuals, so that the company is not brought to a halt on the resignation or death of a shareholder. Limited liability companies have to register their Accounts annually with the Registrar of Companies, together with a Directors' Report and an Annual Bulletin; they must hold an Annual General Meeting.

A company becomes registered as a Public Limited Company (PLC) when it has at least £50,000 authorised share capital. It is then required to use PLC after its name.

8.3.4   Memorandum and Articles of Association

The Memorandum of Association and Articles of Association are drawn up when a limited company is formed. The Memorandum stipulates the Company's objectives (its main trading reasons) and the Articles lay down the rules for the operation of the company, often including the broad areas in which it is going to trade.

9.1 Business cards

These are usually about 3½″ × 2″ and are engraved following the house style.

They should show the name of the representative, his or her job title, the name, address and telephone number of the firm and its FAX and Telex numbers if appropriate *(See 3.6 and 3.19)*.

9.2 Compliments slips

These should be printed with the same information as the company letter heading with the words 'With Compliments' in addition. They are used as a way of showing who the sender is (of a report or an invoice, for example) when a covering letter is unnecessary.

9.3 Computer stationery and materials

9.3.1 Stationery
For ordinary cut sheet paper see 9.4.1.

Continuous stationery This comes in two main types:

- With guide holes in a strip down each side of the paper. The strip is torn off after the paper has been used.
- Lightly glued to a backing sheet which itself has guide holes to feed it through the printer. The fair copy is quite easily detached from the backing sheet.

Printout paper is available with carbons interleaved (OTC) or without carbons (NCR). Printers can normally take up to two sheets of paper plus a carbon.

Labels These are available on continuous stationery or on individual A4 sheets. They are self-adhesive and pre-cut. It may be cheaper to print one copy of each sheet of labels needed and then to use that printout to make photocopies on further sheets of labels.

9.3.2 Materials
Binders These are available in a great variety of designs for storing printouts.

Cleaning materials   Anti-static cleaning materials are used for screens, disk drive heads, keyboards, hard disks, printers etc.

Pens   Using a pen with a tip that retracts if you press too hard helps to prevent damage to disks. (It is better to fill in the disk label before sticking it on the disk *(See 3.2)*.)

Printwheels   The four things to consider when choosing a print wheel are the range of characters, the typeface, the pitch, and whether metal or plastic is required.

Ribbons   There are two main types of ribbon: fabric and multi-strike (carbon). The carbon ones can only be used once and are therefore less economical, although cheaper to buy. The fabric ones can be used until they are too faint for the work you are doing.

Although multistrike ribbons give a better finish, if there is a lot of emboldening in the work and you want to make photocopies of it afterwards, it can be better to use a new fabric ribbon. Photocopies can turn out blurred if the ink on the original is very dark. *(See 1.6)*

Storage   Correct storage of disks is very important – not only to protect them from damage by fire or smoke but also for security reasons. If you would not leave the paper copy lying around, then the disk should similarly be locked away. *(See 3.2)*

9.4   Paper and envelopes

9.4.1   Paper
Common sizes:

A3	297mm × 420mm (11¾″ × 16½″)
A4	210mm × 297mm (8¼″ × 11¾″)
A5	210mm × 148mm (8¼″ × 5⅝″)
Foolscap	203mm × 330mm (8″ × 13″)

Portrait: shorter sides at the top and bottom
Landscape: longer sides at the top and bottom
Weights of paper are given in grammes per square metre (gsm).

Grades: Quality writing paper is usually 100gsm in weight.
NCR (No Carbon Required) paper is multiset paper: you write on the top copy, and what you have written is also imprinted on the underneath copies
Bond: for letters and continuation sheets (80gsm)
Bank: for carbon copies
Duplicating paper: differs according to the method of duplication

Carbon paper:	Number of copies
Super heavyweight	1– 2
Heavyweight	1– 3
Standard weight	4– 6
Manifold	7–10
Supermanifold	11–15

Amount: Paper is usually sold by the ream, which is 480 or 500 sheets. It is odd, but true, that some people quote 480 sheets to the ream, and others 500.

9.4.2 Envelopes

Post Office Preferred POP sizes are as follows:
not more than 6mm (¼″) thick
no smaller than 90mm × 140mm (3½″ × 5½″)
no longer than 120mm × 235mm (4¾″ × 9¼″)
made from paper of at least 63gsm

The two standard sizes of envelope which conform to the POP sizes are:
C6 114mm × 162mm (4½″ × 6⅜″)
DL (for A4 letters) 110mm × 220mm (4¼″ × 8⅝″)

Bankers:

Board backed:	for keeping things flat, e.g. photographs
Internal:	for using several times
Manilla:	extra strong, usually brown
Padded:	for protecting the contents, e.g. cassette
Pocket:	opening on the short side
Security lock:	with slits in the flaps to prevent the envelope being opened undetected
Wallet:	opening on the long side
Window:	with a covered cut-out panel to save typing the address on the envelope

9.5 Stock control

The important thing about being in charge of stock control is to know the position of stock at any one time so as to avoid running out when people might need something from the stores. In order not to run out, but also not to have unnecessary amounts in stock, it is best to keep some sort of record system.

The simplest sort of record system requires *requisition forms*, for people to make their orders on, and *stock control cards* which show how much has been ordered, how much received and how much is left.

9.5.1 Requisition forms

The minimum of information that a requisition form is likely to include is:

- a description of the item
- the quantity required
- the person/department making the order
- date
- authorisation (if necessary)

A simple requisition form might look like this:

STATIONERY REQUISITION			
Name:	*Dept.:*	*Date:*	
Quantity	*Size*	*Description*	*Colour*
Signature:		*Authorisation:*	

9.5.2 Stock control cards

These are used for recording the amounts of each item received from a supplier and the amounts issued. Also, each card should show the present balance. A typical stock card might look like this:

STOCK RECORD CARD					
Description	Plain Typing Paper			*Size*	A4
Unit	Reams	*Type*	Bond	*Colour*	White
	Maximum 50			*Minimum* 10	
Date	*Received*		*Supplier*	*Issued*	*Balance*

The maximum level is the most you should need to hold in stock; the minimum level is the least you can hold without danger of running out. If the balance reaches the minimum level, that is the time to re-order from the supplier.

9.5 Stock control

If no maximum or minimum levels have been established then they can be worked out by keeping a record of how much of each item is requested by departments over a few months.

Each new balance is arrived at by adding the quantity received from the previous balance, or by subtracting the quantity given out from the previous balance.

9.5.3 Stocktaking

This is done, usually once a year, for a number of reasons, mainly to assess the value of the company. It also provides a useful point at which to check the record cards against the stock actually held. Ideally the balance should correspond to the stock held. If it does not, this will show up at the stocktaking.

A stocktaking list for stationery might follow this format:

Stock at .... [date]				
Description	*Unit*	*Quantity held*	*Price*	*Value*
Plain white A4 Bond typing paper	Reams			
Plain white A4 Bank typing paper	Reams			
White pocket envelopes	Packets			
Black typewriter ribbons	Ones			

The price entered for each item should be cost price or current selling price, whichever is the lower. By multiplying the quantity by the price for each item the total value of stock held can be calculated.

10.1   Advice Note

An Advice Note is sent by the supplier advising the receiver that goods are due to arrive. The Note is usually sent separately, e.g. by post when the goods are sent by carrier.

10.2   Air Waybill

This is a sort of aviation Bill of Lading *(See 10.4)*. It is a contract of carriage when goods are sent by air, and acts as a receipt for the goods. It is made out by the airline.

10.3   Bill of Exchange

This is an Order in writing addressed by one person to another, signed by the person giving it. It is not an Order for goods *(See 10.12)*, but requires the person to whom it is addressed to pay, on demand or on a future date (known or to be fixed), a specific sum to the person who has signed the order, to a third person or to the bearer of the document. For example a supplier could supply goods and send a Bill of Exchange to the receiver requiring the receiver to pay on a given date. The receiver of the goods signs the Bill to acknowledge the debt, and the Bill is legal proof of the debt. It is often used when payment is to be delayed.

    It can be 'discounted' with a bank, i.e. if the supplier wanted the money early, the bank would pay the amount, less a discount for its services, and the receiver of the goods still pays on the due date. The bank is acting as a bridge.

10.4   Bill of Lading

This is the receipt given by a Ship's Master to a consignor of goods, stating in detail the goods loaded on board the ship. The Bill of Lading, like the Air Waybill *(See 10.2)*, is an important part of the papers which travel with goods being imported or exported.

10.5   Credit Note

A Credit Note is issued by a supplier of goods when goods are

−returned as faulty
−not delivered for some reason.

Usually the goods have already been invoiced and a Credit Note will correct the original sale.

In dealing with the public a Credit Note is treated as money when redeemed by the customer, e.g. goods are returned to a shop, a Credit Note is issued, and the customer encashes that Note when making the next purchase.

In business a Credit Note reduces the amount to be paid by the purchaser, either on the current Invoice *(See 10.11)* or the next one.

10.1 Advice Note
10.2 Air Waybill
10.3 Bill of Exchange
10.4 Bill of Lading
10.5 Credit Note
10.6 Consignment Note
10.7 Customs Declaration

10.6 Consignment Note

A Consignment Note is very like a Delivery Note *(See 10.8)* in that it goes *with* the goods, detailing the goods in that consignment. It is often used when the consignment consists of several packages; the number of packages is listed, but not necessarily the contents of each.

10.7 Customs Declaration

All goods being sent abroad, with the exception of newspapers and printed matter, must be accompanied by a Customs Declaration.

−For small items, sent personally, a Customs Declaration Form can be obtained from the Post Office.
−For export purposes the system is much more complicated, and companies should first check HM Customs and Excise *Tariff and Overseas Trade Classification Book* to ascertain the correct classification for the goods.
There are then various ways of declaring the goods, and advice should be sought from the local Customs office. Refer to *Customs Notice 275* of September 1981.
−For import purposes refer to *Public Notice 465*; the most common form used in importing is Form C10.

10.8 Delivery Note

Like a Consignment Note *(See 10.6)*, the Delivery Note goes *with* the goods. The Delivery Note usually gives great detail of what is being delivered, and is based on the original Order *(See 10.12)*. It will sometimes have marked on it goods which are 'to follow'.

When goods arrive at the purchaser's premises, they should be checked against the Delivery Note and any discrepancies noted. The purchaser will be invoiced *(See 10.11)* by the supplier according to the goods checked off on the Delivery Note.

Delivery 'Notes' may be on floppy disk.

10.9   Estimate

An Estimate (e.g. given by a builder) is a note of what the work is *likely* to cost, if no unforeseen expenditure arises. It is not as firm as a Quotation *(See 10.16)*. An estimate is usually given free of charge.

10.10   Insurance

Insurance of goods in transit is not a legal requirement; the responsibility for insuring the goods rests with the owners. Ownership of goods can sometimes vary; e.g. an exporter normally owns the goods at least until they are in the docks or airport or on board the transit vessel (ship or plane). Thereafter the ownership may pass to the purchaser of the goods at various stages.

There are various ways of arranging this, but whatever the method of insurance, a Certificate of Insurance is an important part of the documents accompanying goods in transit.

10.11   Invoice

An Invoice is the official 'bill' for goods received (except when it is a Shipping document *(see 10.19)*). An Invoice should bear:

 – the supplier's name and address
 – the customer's name and address
 – the Invoice number
 – the date
 – the quantity and description of goods or services supplied
 – the total excluding VAT
 – the VAT charged *(See 7.9)*
 – the supplier's VAT number
 – any discount or allowance made
 – payment terms (e.g. 30 days net)

When received, and before payment, an Invoice should be checked against the original Order *(See 10.12)* and against the Delivery Note *(See 10.8)* to make sure the goods or services charged for were actually ordered and received.

10.8	Delivery Note
10.9	Estimate
10.10	Insurance
10.11	Invoice
10.12	Order
10.13	Payment

10.12   Order

An Order is a document raised by the purchaser to order goods or services from a supplier. An Order should contain:

- the name and address of the purchaser
- the name and address of the supplier
- the quantity and description of the goods
- the address for the delivery of the goods
- the address to which the Invoice is to be sent
  any special requirements (e.g. latest acceptable delivery date)
- the number of the order, if done on an official form

10.13   Payment

See Banking services (7.3).

Payment may be made by:

- cash
- cheque
- credit card
- credit transfer
- voucher
- banker's order
- computer transfer of funds
- standing order with a bank
- direct debit
- standing order with a credit card company
- postal order etc.

When payment is made, always make a note of when it was done, the amount paid, what the payment was for, details of the payment method (e.g. cheque number) etc., so that the payment can be traced if necessary.

10.14   Price list

This is, obviously, a list of prices of goods or services which can be supplied. Check:

–that the price list is current
–discount for quantity
–whether or not price includes VAT *(See 7.9)*
–exact description of goods or services

The most important item on a price list is the date.

10.15   Pro forma invoice

Used mainly for import/export, the Pro forma Invoice gives full details of goods offered. The importer abroad can use the Pro forma Invoice to apply for all the necessary import documents *(See 10.19)*.
Prices are usually quoted as:

–CIF (Cost Insurance Freight) plus name of destination: price covers cost of goods, insurance and freight (transport) to that port.
–C&F (Cost & Freight): covers cost of transport only (no insurance) *(See 10.10)*.
–FOB (Free on Board): includes cost of delivery to ship at named port plus loading charge only included (no insurance and freight charge thereafter).

10.16   Quotation

This is a firm declaration of what an item or service will cost, e.g. a printer's quotation for 200 Menu Cards. *This is not an estimate (See 10.9)*.
Check delivery dates, payment terms (discount etc.) and whether or not VAT *(See 7.9)* is included.

10.17   Remittance Advice

A note sent by the purchaser to the supplier with the Payment *(See 10.13)* giving details of what the payment is for (advising of the remittance).
Suppliers often attach a Remittance Advice to an Invoice *(See 10.11)* or a Statement *(See 10.20)* which can be returned with the payment.

When sent with a cheque, a photocopy of an Invoice or a Compliment Slip with a note of the Invoice number and the date is, in effect, a Remittance Advice.

10.18   Requisition

Basically an order *(See 10.12)*, but usually internal to the organisation, e.g. requisitioning supplies from the stationery store.

10.19   Shipping

All imported and exported goods must be accompanied by papers, the most common of which are:

- a Standard Shipping Note; this must accompany all goods sent to the docks and it acts as a receipt from the Port Authorities. It also carries instructions about what to do with the goods.
- an Invoice, which in international trade is not a demand for payment *(See 10.11)* but a record of goods sent.
- a Certificate of Origin in some cases.
- a Packing List, particularly when there are different goods in different cases, rather like a Consignment Note *(See 10.6)*.
- a Customs Declaration *(See 10.7)*.
- an Import Licence, where applicable.
- a Certificate of Insurance *(See 10.10)*.
- an Air Waybill (when sent by air) *(See 10.2)*.
- a Bill of Lading *(See 10.4)*.
- a Movement Certificate in certain circumstances for preferential rates of duty.

10.20   Statement

This is a Statement of Account, e.g. a Bank Statement, Credit Card Statement etc.

It is also a Statement of Invoices sent but not yet paid. Some companies pay only on receipt of a Statement. Some companies do not send Statements. Watch for the title of the document and the terms set out on the original Invoice *(See 10.11)*.

(For abbreviations commonly used on Bank Statements, see 7.2.3.)

11.1   Air travel

11.1.1   Baggage allowances
A certain amount of baggage may be carried on a plane free in the hold or as hand luggage. Items carried in excess of the allowances may be charged for. You should check these details with the airline or travel agent, as allowances may vary according to the type of ticket bought and the country of destination.

Hand luggage   It is important to check the number of pieces of hand luggage permitted. The dimensions of any such luggage must fall within certain limits, usually 115cm (45″) in total. This means that the length, width and depth together must not equal more than 115cm (45″). The weight limit for any piece of hand luggage is usually 5kg.

The following articles are generally not counted as baggage:

–handbag
–coat
–umbrella
–camera
–binoculars
–reading material
–duty free purchases

Hold luggage   The amount of luggage that can be taken in the hold is set either by weight or by pieces of certain maximum dimensions. The weight limit is usually 20kg or 30kg depending on the class of the ticket. The maximum total dimensions allowed for one piece are usually 158cm (62″).

Each of the following articles generally counts as one piece of baggage:

–snow skis
–golf bag with clubs
–surfboard
–rucksack

11.1.2 Connections

A car can be hired to meet a traveller at an airport. This can sometimes be arranged through the airline. Alternatively, most airports operate their own bus services to city centres and a train or underground link may also be a possibility.

| 11.1 | Air travel |
| 11.2 | Car hire |

Most scheduled and charter flights to Switzerland offer a service whereby the traveller's luggage is automatically taken to the eventual rail or coach destination. For example, if you are flying to Zürich and taking a train from there to Bern the luggage will be automatically checked through and you will pick it up in Bern, not having to see it on to the train yourself.

11.1.3 Domestic

There are a number of shuttle services between major UK cities. Savings can be made by buying a ticket at least 14 days in advance. However, it is possible to buy a ticket on the plane itself or any time before checking in – and the latest checking in time is 10 mins before take-off (if you only have hand luggage of which the dimensions do not exceed 115mm (45″)). No reservation is necessary.

Details of flights and fares are available on Oracle, Ceefax and Prestel systems *(See 3.11 and 3.18)*.

11.1.4 International

Information on flights and fares is available from a number of sources: travel agents, airlines, Oracle, Ceefax and Prestel, and the *ABC World Airways Guide* which is published monthly.

11.2 Car hire

11.2.1 Charges

Rates quoted by car hire companies usually exclude VAT and petrol. Rental from a UK company, even for journeys abroad, will be payable in sterling. A deposit is usually required, calculated on the basis of the estimated charges, which is then deducted from the final bill. Cars are grouped into price bands. If the model requested is not available the usual practice is to provide another model from the same group or, if this is not possible, to provide one from a higher band at no extra charge.

11.2.2   Chauffeurs
Meal and subsistence allowances are payable for chauffeurs, depending on the length of the hire period. A supplement may be charged for Bank Holiday hire.

11.2.3   Collection and delivery
Some companies will charge a supplement for this service.

11.2.4   Insurance
Unlimited cover of public liability for damage to property and passenger liability will usually be automatically included in the charges. The customer may be required to pay a certain amount towards damage or loss of the vehicle through fire or theft. It is possible to avoid this contribution charge on payment of a non-returnable waiver fee before the hire begins. A more comprehensive Personal Accident Insurance is not issued automatically by the hire firm but may be bought from them.

11.2.5   Minicabs
For frequent short trips most businesses will have a single firm which they use regularly and with whom they have a company account. Bookings then require a single phone call. The secretary may need to keep a record of the date, purpose and person for whom the minicab was hired and of who made the booking.

11.2.6   One way journeys
Most companies offer the service where a car may be picked up from one place and returned to another. This may even be possible across countries. A 'drop-off' charge may be made.

11.2.7   Payment
All the major credit cards are usually acceptable. If a firm is to be used often then it is probably possible to open a company account with them. Firms may also, on request, issue a number of their own credit cards to those in the business likely to make use of them. Such a card can sometimes be used to claim discounts, to speed up the booking process or to ensure petrol at designated garages in times of a shortage. If payment is not made by credit card or charge card then a deposit is payable in advance.

11.2.8   Rail/Drive
This is a service offered by certain companies where the customer

picks up the car from a major British Rail station. This service is free during normal office hours.

11.2.9   *Restrictions*
Most companies stipulate that the driver must have held a full licence for a minimum of 1 year. Licences which bear endorsements are accepted at the company's discretion. Many companies also stipulate a minimum age, usually between 18 and 25. Those in the youngest age group eligible to drive a hired car may also be restricted as to the type of car they may drive, and purchase of the waiver *(see 11.2.4)* may be compulsory.

11.2.10   *Shuttle/Drive*
This is where all arrangements are made before the flight through the airline so that on landing the customer may go straight to the waiting car without the need for any more paperwork.

11.2.11   *Driving abroad*
For driving abroad an International Driving Permit may be necessary. Some countries specify a minimum age and clean driving licence held for a certain minimum period.

Where the current insurance policy does not cover foreign travel a Green Card may be necessary. For example, if the car is comprehensively insured in the UK but only for third party abroad, purchase of the Green Card will extend the full insurance to foreign travel. This is best obtained through the usual insurance company.

Information on the above, on legal requirements when driving abroad (e.g. carrying a hazard triangle) and suggested routes is available from the AA or RAC.

11.3   Checklists

For the secretary

- Vaccinations arranged as necessary *(see 11.9)*;
- Visa(s) and passport(s) in order *(see 11.8 and 11.10)*;
- Insurance arranged *(see 11.6)*;
- Confirm hotel and travel bookings *(see 11.5)*;
- Cheques and cash obtained *(see 11.4)*;
- Make copies of all documents to be used;

- Make copies of the itinerary. Keep one and send others to those who need one *(see 11.7)*;
- List of all telephone, telex and fax numbers for contact in an emergency.

For the traveller

- Credit cards *(see 11.4.1)*
- Documents to be used
- Foreign currency *(see 11.4.3)*
- Itinerary *(see 11.7)*
- Keys
- List of numbers of Travellers' Cheques (kept separately from the cheques) *(see 11.4.5)*
- Medicines
- Passport *(see 11.8)*
- Sterling
- Telephone numbers needed in an emergency (e.g. of the bank to report lost/stolen cards)
- Tickets
- Travellers' Cheques *(see 11.4.5)*
- Vaccination certificate *(see 11.9)*
- Insurance documents (e.g. 'Green Card' and policy documents) *(see 11.6)*
- Driving Licence (plus International Driving Permit if required) *(see 11.2.11)*

11.4   Foreign currency and Travellers' Cheques

Some countries restrict the amount that can be taken in and out of the country. Details can be obtained from banks.

11.4.1   Credit cards
The major credit cards can be used in Europe and some other countries. They can be used to make purchases or as cash cards for withdrawing local currency.

11.4.2   Eurocheques
These work in the same way as ordinary cheques on a current account backed by a Eurocheque card. The difference is that the cheque can be written for an amount in currencies other than sterling. The amount of the cheque is converted into sterling by the

issuing bank and deducted from the
current account in the normal way.
Each cheque can be written for up to a
specified amount, usually £100 or the
local currency equivalent.

One advantage of Eurocheques is
that the drawer pays for them as they
are used, not in advance as for
Travellers' Cheques. However, there may be an annual charge for
the Eurocheque card and a charge for each cheque drawn. In
addition, a handling charge may be made by the foreign bank which
processes the cheque. This may be payable either when the cheque
is cashed, or deducted later from the account by the issuing bank.

The Eurocheque card can also be used in some countries as a cash
card to withdraw cash or order new Eurocheques.

11.4.3   Foreign currency
Small change can be vital on arrival in a foreign country for such
things as fares or phone calls, therefore it is wise to order a small
amount of the currency of each country at least 1 week in advance of
the day of departure. The issuer of the currency will charge a
commission for the service.

11.4.4   Open credit
If a traveller is going to spend some time in one town abroad it may
be worth arranging an open credit with the bank. This is where the
British branch makes a special arrangement with the nominated
bank abroad so that the traveller is offered the same facilities by the
foreign bank as if it were his or her local branch.

11.4.5   Travellers' Cheques
The traveller buys cheques up to a certain amount in the currency of
the country to be visited. Cheques in a foreign currency should be
ordered in advance. Sterling Travellers' Cheques can usually be
obtained more quickly, but payment for them may have to be made
in cash.

Some establishments will accept Travellers' Cheques in payment
as if they were ordinary cheques, but as each cheque will be for a
pre-specified amount only this is not usually a practical way of
making small purchases.

A commission is usually charged when buying the cheques and
also when cashing them. The advantage of Travellers' Cheques is

that it is a safer way of carrying money than taking cash abroad. Foreign banks will require proof of identity when cashing the cheques. Unused cheques can be sold back to issuer on return.

The traveller should make a note of the cheque numbers and also of the emergency number to ring if the cheques are lost or stolen. These details should be kept separately from the cheques themselves.

11.5   Hotel and travel bookings

11.5.1   *Hotel bookings*
Sources of information about hotels:

- AA and RAC books
- *ABC Rail Guide* (Britain only)
- *Where To Stay* the English Tourist Board guide (Britain only)
- *Hotels and Restaurants of Britain* the British Hotels Restaurants and Caterers Association Guide
- *The Good Hotel Guide* (Britain and Western Europe)
- *Egon Ronay guide* (Britain and Eire)
- *Arthur Eperon's guide* (Britain only)
- *Hotels and Restaurants* British Tourist Association guide
- *The Financial Times World Hotel Directory* (international)
- *ABC Hotel Guide* (Britain and international)
- travel agents
- some car hire firms and airlines

When confirming a hotel booking you should state all the relevant details:

- name(s) of person(s) visiting
- name of the company
- day and date of arrival
- day and date of departure
- length of stay
- type of room and facilities required (e.g. private bath)
- whether any meals are required
- the approximate time of arrival

11.5.2   *Travel bookings*
There are books available on the customs of other countries which could prove a good investment for the business traveller. Local

libraries usually have a selection of leaflets providing hints to exporters and travellers.

Tickets may be bought directly from the transport company (e.g. BR) or through a travel agent. They will also be able to advise on the length of time in advance that bookings should be

| 11.4 | Foreign currency and Travellers' Cheques |
| 11.5 | Hotel and travel bookings |

made. Unless buying the ticket a day or less before departure any booking made by phone should be confirmed in writing. All the details on the tickets need to be checked when they are received. *(For car hire see 11.2.)*

11.5.3 Rail travel

Rail travel within the UK For detailed information on fares, times and different services see the *ABC Rail Guide*. Information is also available from BR direct and on Prestel *(see 3.11)*. Prestel also offers a booking facility.

The main services which are relevant to business travellers are:

- Motorail – where the traveller's car is also taken on the train.
- Sleeper tickets – 1st or 2nd class tickets are available for overnight journeys. This service is not suitable for those using wheelchairs.
- Intercity Executive – this ticket includes 1st class return travel, reservation and 24 hours' free parking at certain stations. BR advise that bookings should be made before 1700 on the day before departure.
- Pullman trains – these offer a luxury service on certain routes. Executive tickets are valid for Pullman travel.
- Short Breaks – these include hotel accommodation for 1 night (or longer) and can be cheaper than a return ticket for the same day.

Rail travel in Europe See *Cook's Continental Timetable*

Rail travel outside Europe See *ABC Air/Rail Europe and Middle East Guide*

11.6 Insurance

Insurance policies are available from travel agents, insurance companies, insurance brokers and banks. (Credit card companies sometimes offer free travel insurance to their customers.) It is usually simplest to arrange a policy through whoever is making the travel arrangements.

Even if the traveller is already insured under a company policy, you should check that the cover extends to the country to be visited and the mode of transport. For example, if someone is insured to drive a company car does that cover taking the car to a different country? Insurance may be needed to cover any or all of these:

- lost/stolen belongings
- delayed baggage
- physical injury or death
- medical care
- third party insurance
- flight delays
- taking a vehicle abroad – 'Green Card' (International Motor Insurance Certificate – *see* **11.2.11**.)

11.7 Itineraries

Points to take into account when organising an itinerary:

- Business hours and shop opening hours may vary according to the country or the area;
- Connections between airports, stations, and meeting points should be borne in mind: how will they be made and how long will they take?
- Holidays, both local and national;
- Time differences.

A typical layout of an itinerary might be as follows:

Mon 3 Jan	Dep. Heathrow flight BA 960 to Marseille 1835 hours (arr. 2100 hours)	Hotel Figaro
Tue 4 Jan	In Marseille	
Wed 5 Jan	Dep. Marseille train 1800 hours to Salon (arr. 2005 hours)	Hotel l'Empire
Thur 6 Jan	Dep. Salon train 1740 hours to Avignon (arr. 1850 hours)	Hotel Cloche

11.8   Passports

It is advisable to check the expiry dates of the passports of those who will be travelling abroad well in advance of the business trip. It takes a minimum of 2 weeks for the Passport Office to process an application outside holiday

periods and longer within holiday periods. Application forms for passports are available from all main Post Offices.

For a British citizen a passport is needed for travel everywhere except the Republic of Ireland. A visitor's passport will suffice for travel to the EEC, and this can be obtained from a main Post Office.

Member countries of the EEC are:

- Belgium
- Denmark
- France
- Federal Republic of Germany
- Greece
- Irish Republic
- Italy
- Luxembourg
- Netherlands
- Portugal
- Spain
- United Kingdom

11.9   Vaccinations

Disease	Risk areas	Vaccination	Certificate?	Time in advance
Cholera	Africa, Asia Middle East	2 injections by doctor	Some countries may require one. Check.	
Polio	Everywhere exc. Europe, N. America, New Zealand & Australia	3 doses of drops taken at 4–8 week intervals	No	2–4 mths

Disease	Risk areas	Vaccination	Certificate?	Time in advance
Typhoid	As for polio	2 injections at an interval of 4–6 wks. Can be reduced to 10 days if unavoidable.	No	2–6 wks
Yellow Fever	Africa, S. America	1 at a YF Vaccination Centre 10 days in advance	Yes, even if you have only passed through a risk area.	10 days

If a traveller had the required injections for a previous trip, you should nevertheless check that no boosters are needed.

Other diseases against which precautions should be taken, although not in the form of vaccinations, include:

– infectious hepatitis
– malaria (anti-malarial tablets are available)
– rabies
– tetanus

More information about the precautions that must be taken when travelling abroad is available from doctors, the Embassy of the country to be visited, British Airways Passenger Immunisation and Medical Centre, and leaflet SA35 issued by the DHSS.

Some vaccinations are free under the NHS; others may have to be paid for. Doctors are entitled to charge for signing or filling in a vaccination certificate.

11.10   Visas

Visas are not needed for trips of under 3 months to countries within the EEC if the traveller has a British passport. *(For a list of EEC members see 11.8.)*

To find out whether a visa is needed to visit a particular country you could telephone the Embassy of that country or ask the travel agent who is making the travel arrangements. This should be done well in advance of the journey as applications may take time to process.

12.1   Conversion tables

Length

1 millimetre	= 1000 micrometres	= 0.0394 inch
1 centimetre	= 10 millimetres	= 0.3937 inch
1 metre	= 100 centimetres	= 1.0936 yards
1 kilometre	= 1000 metres	= 0.6214 mile
1 inch		= 2.54 centimetres
1 foot	= 12 inches	= 30.48 centimetres
1 yard	= 36 inches	= 0.9144 metre
1 mile	= 1760 yards	= 1.6093 kilometres

Area

1 sq. metre	= 10,000 sq. centimetres	= 1.1906 sq. yards
1 hectare	= 10,000 sq. metres	= 2.4711 acres
1 sq. kilometre	= 100 hectares	= 0.3861 sq. mile
1 sq. foot	= 144 sq. inches	= 0.0929 sq. metre
1 sq. yard	= 9 sq. feet	= 0.8361 sq. metre
1 acre	= 4840 sq. yards	= 4046.9 sq. metres

Capacity

1 litre	= 1 cubic decimetre	= 0.22 gallon

(A litre of water is a pint and three quarters)

1 cubic yard	= 27 cubic feet	= 0.7646 cubic metre
1 pint	= 4 gills	= 0.5683 litre
1 gallon	= 8 pints	= 4.5461 litres

Weight

1 gramme	= 1000 milligrammes	= 0.0353 ounce
1 kilogramme	= 1000 grammes	= 2.2046 pounds
1 tonne	= 1000 kilogrammes	= 0.9842 ton
1 ounce	= 437.5 grains	= 28.35 grammes
1 pound	= 16 ounces	= 0.4536 kilogrammes
1 stone	= 14 pounds	= 6.35 kilogrammes
1 ton	= 2240 pounds	= 1.016 tonnes

Temperature conversion

To convert Fahrenheit to Celsius:

Take 32 from Fahrenheit figure; multiply by 5 and divide by 9

To convert Celsius to Fahrenheit:

Divide Celsius figure by 5 and multiply by 9; add 32.

12.2 Copyright

Copyright is a form of ownership. There are two types of copyright.

The author's copyright This is copyright of the literary or artistic work itself. The holder of the copyright is indicated in the front of the book or paper by this sign ©, followed by the holder's name and the date. This form of copyright lasts for the author's lifetime and for 50 years after his or her death.

The publisher's copyright This is copyright of the typographical arrangement of the work. This belongs to the publisher of the edition and lasts for 25 years from the date of that edition.

Permission to reproduce any part of a work may be sought from the author (usually via the publisher) or under a blanket licence. Blanket licences are usually granted to educational institutions because it would be impractical for them to seek individual permission each time. Blanket licences are granted via the Copyright Licensing Agency.

The statute which sets out the law on copyright is the Copyright Act 1956.

12.3 Correction signs

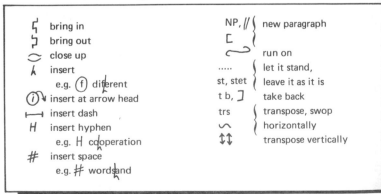

12.4 Currency denominations

*For calculating currency conversion
see 7.1.1.*

For current exchange rates check with
newspapers, banks, Building Societies
or Travel Agents.

12.4.1 Major national currencies

Country	Currency	Country	Currency
Albania	Lek	Greece	Drachma
Argentina	Peso	Guatemala	Quetzal
Australia	Dollar	Guyana	Dollar
Austria	Schilling		
		Haiti	Gourde
Belgium/Luxemburg	Franc	Honduras Rep	Lempira
Belize	Dollar	Hong Kong	Dollar
Bolivia	Peso Boliviano	Iceland	Króna
		India	Rupee
Botswana	Pula	Indonesia	Rupiah
Brazil	Cruzeiro	Iran	Rial
Bulgaria	Lev	Iraq	Dinar
Burma	Kyat	Israel	Pound
		Italy	Lira
Canada	Dollar		
Chile	Peso	Jamaica	Dollar
China	Yuan	Japan	Yen
Colombia	Peso	Jordan	Dinar
Costa Rica	Colón		
Cuba	Peso	Kenya	K Shilling
Czechoslovakia	Koruna		
		Lebanon	Pound
Denmark	Krone		
Dominican Rep	Peso	Malaysia	Ringgit
		Mexico	Peso
Ecuador	Sucre	Morocco	Dirham
Egypt	Pound		
Eire	Punt	Netherlands	Guilder
El Salvador	Colón	New Zealand	Dollar
Ethiopia	Dollar	Nicaragua	Cordoba
		Nigeria	Naira
Finland	Markka	Norway	Krone
France	Franc		
		Pakistan	Rupee
Germany (E.)	Mark	Panama	Balboa
Germany (W.)	D Mark	Paraguay	Guarani

Country	Currency	Country	Currency
Peru	Sol	Tunisia	Dinar
Philippines	Peso	Turkey	Lira
Poland	Zloty	United Arab	
Portugal	Escudo	Emirates	Dirham
Romania	Leu	United Kingdom	Pound
		USA	Dollar
South Africa	Rand	USSR	Rouble
Spain	Peseta	Uruguay	Peso
Sri Lanka	Rupee		
Swaziland	Malangeni	Venezuela	Bolivar
Sweden	Krona	Yugoslavia	Dinar
Switzerland	Franc	Yemen Arab Rep	Riyal
Syria	Pound	Yemen South	Dinar
Tanzania	T Shilling	Zaire	Zaire
Thailand	Baht	Zambia	Kwacha
Trinidad & Tobago	T T Dollar	Zimbabwe	Dollar

12.5   Press guide

12.5.1   Terms

Classified   This is the cheapest form of advertising available in a publication. There is no element of display in the classified section and the charge is normally per word or per line. Such advertisements can often be dictated over the telephone for this reason. Usually a certain number of words are emphasised (in blocks, emboldened) free of charge – any others cost extra.

Column inches/centimetres   A newspaper page may have what appear to be several different widths of columns. When a price is quoted per column centimetre or inch it is the price of a centimetre or of an inch down the narrowest column available. The amount of space taken up is measured down the page in centimetres or inches.

Display   These are the largest advertisements which may take anything from ¹⁄₁₆ of a page to a whole page. They can incorporate different typefaces, logos, drawings etc.

Semi-display   As the word implies, this sort of advertisement is halfway to full display. There is usually a box drawn around each one – this explains the higher charge because the advertiser has to pay for the space taken up by the box. The advantage of this sort of display is that it is more likely to catch the reader's eye.

12.5.2 Advertising

When deciding which publication(s) to use, points to bear in mind include:

12.4	Currency denominations
12.5	Press guide
12.6	Quarter Days

- the type of publication, i.e. who reads it, how often it is published
- the length of time in advance that space can be booked
- the price
- the length of time in advance that the copy will have to be delivered

Having decided to place an advertisement in a particular publication and under which heading it is to go (Secretarial, Legal etc.) it is necessary to compile a checklist of things that must be included. Here is an example checklist for an advertisement for a secretarial post:

- job title
- salary/rate of pay
- hours, if unusual
- location of job
- minimum qualifications and/or experience required
- method of reply, e.g. application form, letter with CV
- closing date for applications
- contact name, address and/or telephone number

12.5.3 Sources of information

- *Benn's Media Directory* gives lists and classifications of all UK newspapers and periodicals and other media
- *Pims Media Directory* is a directory of types of publication, published monthly
- *Willings Press Guide* is a yearly directory of publications in Europe, America, Australasia, Middle and Far East
- *British Rates and Data* (Brad), published monthly, gives information on current charges, copy dates and types of advertisement taken in all UK papers.

12.6 Quarter days

12.6.1 England, Wales and Ireland

Lady Day   25 March

Midsummer Day	24 June
Michaelmas Day	29 September
Christmas Day	25 December

12.6.2   *Scotland*

Candlemas	2 February
Whitsunday	15 May
Lammas	1 August
Martinmas	11 November

12.7   Reference sources

Reference libraries will normally have reference books on almost every specific business area, e.g. medical, legal, export etc. The list below is of more general sources of information.

12.7.1   *Business books*

Directory of Directors   List of Directors and their Directorships; list of Companies and their Directors.

Kelly's Business Directory   Classified Trades and Professions; a little like Yellow Pages *(See 12.7.4)* but nationwide.

Kompass   Directors of Companies by product and by company in the UK and various European countries.

Thomas Register   The same sort of thing as Kompass, but for the USA.

Who Owns Whom   Directory of which companies own which others, e.g. subsidiaries and associates.

Who's Who   Directory of prominent people in the UK and abroad with their achievements, titles and hobbies.

12.7.2   *Electronic databases*

For Ceefax, Prestel and Oracle, for weather, travel and business information, see Unit 3.

12.7.3   *General reference books*

Burke's Peerage   Lists of nobility in the UK and abroad; gives useful forms of address.

Debrett's Peerage   Similar to Burke's Peerage.

Diaries   Often have mileage charts, conversion tables, time zones etc.

Dod's Parliamentary Companion   potted biographies of current

MPs, parliamentary terms and forms of address.

Gazetteer Geographical index or dictionary: list of countries, towns, rivers etc. with information about them.

Hansard Record of daily happenings in Parliament.

Newspapers Currency rates, stock exchange rates, theatre and other entertainments, weather, etc.

Vacher's Parliamentary Companion Published quarterly, this gives the names of members of the House of Commons and the House of Lords, judges, lobby journalists and who holds which ministerial office.

12.7.4 Telephone and Post Office books

Business Telephone Book List of local businesses by trade and profession, e.g. Office Services.

The Phone Book (the Telephone Directory) Directory of all local phone users, but also gives information on:

–local BT area
–BT services
–useful local numbers (hospitals, transport etc.)
–correct postal addresses
–national and international dialling codes, etc.

Post Office Guide Guide to all Post Office services.

Thomson's directory of *local* businesses, services, community services etc.

Yellow Pages list of local businesses under trades and professions in alphabetical order.

12.7.5 Travel books
(For travel reference sources see 11.5.)

12.7.6 Word books

Dictionary Words, their meaning and derivation – useful for checking spelling.

Dorland's Pocket Medical Dictionary Published by Saunders.

Dictionary of Synonyms Gives words and similar words with the same meanings.

Encyclopaedia General knowledge; the larger the encyclopaedia the more detailed the information.

Fowler's Modern English Usage   Acknowledged authority on English grammar.

Larousse   Mixture of dictionary and encyclopaedia.

The Layman's Dictionary of English Law   by Gavin McFarlane, published by Waterlow.

Pear's Cyclopaedia   Gives all sorts of everyday information in its 'General Compendium' or 'Desk Top Information' section, e.g. Roman numerals, Greek alphabet, Beaufort wind scale, weights and measures etc.

Thesaurus (treasury)   A sort of dictionary giving alternatives to words; fuller information than a Dictionary of Synonyms.

12.8   Special symbols

Symbol	Meaning	Symbol	Meaning
≃	approximately	<	less than
@	at, at the rate of	≤	less than or equal to
¢	cent(s)	%	per cent
°	degree(s)	‰	per thousand
$	dollar(s)	£	pounds sterling
≠	is not equal to	lb	pounds weight
′	foot, feet	3̇	figure recurs ad infinitum
″	inch(es)	*, ⳹	marks of reference
>	greater than	⳹	if before the name of a
≥	greater than or equal to		person: deceased

12.9   Time zones

For standard times when GMT is 12.00 noon, see map on pages 154–5.

For British Summer Time (Daylight Saving) times add one hour to standard time, whether other time zones are ahead of or behind GMT.

Daylight saving normally runs from March/April to late September/October depending on the time zone. If in doubt, check with travel agents, etc.

12.10   Translation services

12.10.1   *Where to look*
Sources for translation services include:

- The Business Directory
- Yellow Pages
- Translation Agencies
- The Institute of Translating and Interpreters (ITI) (Telephone 01-794 9931)
- The Institute of Linguists (Telephone 01-359 7445)

Each Institute has a register of translators.

12.10.2   *Questions to ask*

- How charges are calculated; this is normally per 1,000 words, but for manuals and complicated material could be a lump sum;
- If charged per 1,000 words, whether that is per 1,000 words of the source language (the language *from* which the translation is to be made) or the target language (the language *into* which the translation is to be made);
- Whether there is any form of quality control of the work;
- To what level, in both languages, the translator has been educated or is proficient;
- Whether the translator has special knowledge of the subject area concerned, e.g. engineering, medical etc.;
- Whether the agency can offer the same translator for the same client, so that there is consistency of work and terminology.

12.10.3   *Interpreters*

- Charges are per day, and the rate depends on the type of work required, e.g. simultaneous translation with headphones, or translating for small groups, etc.
- Interpreters will need to be supplied with papers beforehand, to familiarise themselves with terms used, the subject matter etc.
- Book interpreters well in advance – six months to a year may be necessary.

12.11   24 hour clock

An easy way of translating British time into the 24 hour clock system is to add or subtract 12, e.g.

TIME ZONES

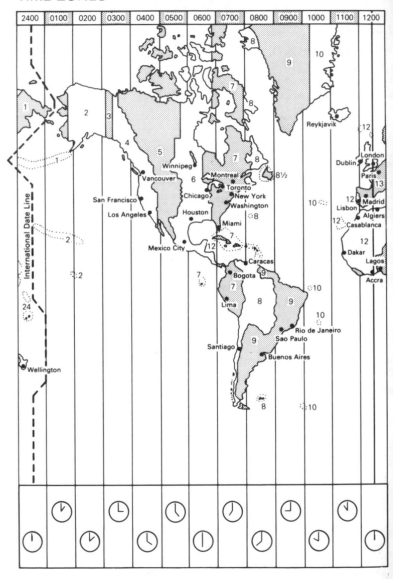

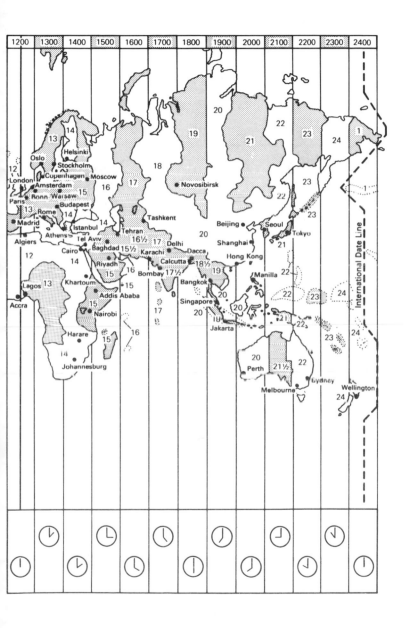

1815 in the 24 hour system translates into 6.15 pm
(18 − 12 = 6)
12.23 pm translates into 2323 in the 24 hour system
(11 + 12 = 23). See drawing below.

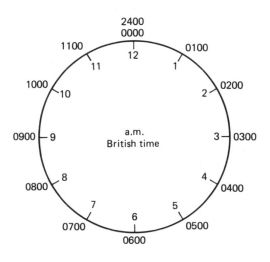

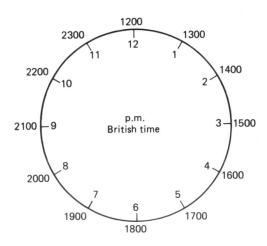

12.12 Useful addresses

12.11 24 hour clock
12.12 Useful
addresses

Advisory, Conciliation and Arbitration Service (ACAS)
Head Office (England and Wales):
Clifton House
Euston Road
LONDON NW1
01-388 5100

Association of British Travel Agents (ABTA)
55 Newman Street
LONDON W1
01-637 2444

Automobile Association (AA)
Look under The Automobile Association in The Phone Book for Regional Headquarters

British Rail Travel Information
Look under British Rail in The Phone Book

Central Office of Information
Hercules Road
LONDON SE1 7DU
01-928 2345

Commission for Racial Equality
Elliott House
10/12 Allington Street
LONDON SW1E 5EH
01-828 7022

Confederation of British Industry (CBI)
Centre Point
103 New Oxford Street
LONDON WC1
01-379 7400

Consumers' Association
14 Buckingham Street
LONDON WC2
01-839 1222

The Daily Telegraph Information Service
01-353 4242

Data Protection Registrar
Springfield House
Water Lane
WILMSLOW
Cheshire SK9 5AX
0625 535777

Department of Employment
Caxton House
Tothill Street
LONDON SW1H 9NF
01-213 3000

EEC Information Unit
8 Story's Gate
LONDON SW1
01-222 8122

Equal Opportunities Commission (EOC)
Overseas House
Quay Street
MANCHESTER M3 3HN
061-833 9244

EOC Scottish Regional Office
249 West George Street
GLASGOW G2 4QE
041-226 4591

EOC Welsh Regional Office
Caerwys House
Windsor Lane
CARDIFF CF1 1B
0222 43552

Office of Fair Trading
Field House
15–25 Breams Buildings
LONDON EC4A 1PR
01-242 2858

Health & Safety Commission and
  Executive Secretariat
Regina House
Old Marylebone Road
LONDON NW1
01-723 1262

**Department of Health and Social
  Security** (Leaflets Unit)
PO Box 21
STANMORE
Middlesex HA7 1AY

The Industrial Society
48 Bryanston Square
LONDON W1
01-262 2401

Board of Inland Revenue
Somerset House
Strand
LONDON WC2R 1LB
01-438 6622

**Institute of Personnel
  Management (IPM)**
35 Camp Road
LONDON SW19
01-946 9100

**London Chamber of Commerce
  and Industry**
69 Cannon Street
LONDON EC4N 5AB
01-248 4444

Manpower Services Commission
Disabled People's Services Branch
Rm W1030
Moorfoot
SHEFFIELD S1 4PQ
0742 703525

Maternity Alliance
59–61 Camden High Street
LONDON NW1 7JL
01-388 6337

The National Computing Centre
Oxford Road
MANCHESTER
M1 7ED
061-228 6333

**Royal Automobile Club
  (RAC)**
RAC House
Lansdowne Road
CROYDON, Surrey
CR9 2JA
01-686 2525

Rights of Women
52–54 Featherstone Street
LONDON EC1Y 8RT
01-251 6575

Department of Trade and Industry
1 Victoria Street
LONDON SW1
01-215 7877

Trades Union Congress (TUC)
Congress House
Great Russell Street
London WC1B 3LS
01-636 4030

**Women Against Sexual
  Harassment (WASH)**
242 Pentonville Road
LONDON N1
01-833 0222

INDEX

Entries in **bold** refer to section headings